Praise for Eleanor Berman's The Cooperating Family . . .

"Practical . . . cheerful."
—*Los Angeles Times*

"Helpful tips . . . good counsel."
—*ALA Booklist*

"[An] excellent handbook for the sharing of family responsibilities."
—*Library Journal*

Grandparenting

a b c's

A BEGINNER'S HANDBOOK

Eleanor Berman

A Perigee Book

A Perigee Book
Published by The Berkley Publishing Group
A division of Penguin Putnam Inc.
375 Hudson Street
New York, NY 10014

Copyright © 1998 by Eleanor Berman
Book design by Tiffany Kukec
Cover design and illustration by Charles R. Björklund

First edition: September 1998

Published simultaneously in Canada.

The Penguin Putnam Inc. World Wide Web site address is
http://www.penguinputnam.com

Library of Congress Cataloging-in-Publication Data

Berman, Eleanor.
Grandparenting ABC's : a beginner's handbook / Eleanor Berman.—
1st. ed.
p.   cm.
"A Perigee Book."
Includes bibliographical references.
ISBN 0-399-52436-3
1. Grandparenting.   2. Grandparent and child.   I. Title.
HQ759.9.B47   1998
306.874'5—dc21   97-52657
CIP

Printed in the United States of America

10   9   8   7   6   5   4   3

For Jackson and his mom,
with thanks to each of you
for the joy you have given me

Contents

Introduction

I am head over heels, hopelessly in love. The object of my affection is on the pudgy side and he isn't much of a conversationalist, but it doesn't matter. When he smiles or takes my hand, my heart turns over and I want to smother him with kisses.

The young man who has captured my heart and changed my life is my first grandchild, Jackson. I was excited at the prospect of becoming a grandparent, but I could never have imagined or anticipated the depth of joy this little boy has brought to me. Jackson is past three now, and the bond grows stronger with every passing day. I know that I am not alone in my feelings about being a grandparent because my friends are also experiencing the same total devotion as they welcome their first grandchildren into their lives.

While later grandchildren will surely claim an equal share of my love, I doubt that I will ever again feel quite the same sense of wonder as I did at his birth—nor will I have the same number of questions. Both before and after my grandson was born, I was constantly being surprised at how much things had changed since I had my children. Right from the start, some of the terminology and technology that goes with pregnancy today was completely new to me. I didn't want or need to read the big, comprehensive books for expectant parents that my daughter was consulting, but I also didn't want to seem hopelessly out-of-date. I went to the library and the bookstore hoping to find a brief, practical book that looked at childbirth, infancy, and the early toddler years from the perspective of a new grandparent, a guide that would tell me what I needed and wanted to know—including the best things to buy for the baby. What I found were cute books of anecdotes about grandparenting, and some very serious books that went all the way into the problems of the teen years, which seemed very far away to me. That's when I decided to write this book. *Grandparenting ABC's* is the book for new grandparents that I wished for but could not find.

I consulted professionals on medical and child development matters, but much of the advice in these pages comes from the real experts—today's parents and grandparents. I started with people I know, moved on to their friends, canvassed people in a large New York ad agency, and discovered the Internet as a fabulous way to reach people all across the country. Both generations have generously shared their experiences on everything from how to get along better with in-laws to which toys, books, and baby gear their families like best. I was truly moved by the beautiful emotions they shared on what the first child or grandchild has meant to them.

My book outline expanded, however, as I reached more people and discovered that some experiences were more complicated than I had anticipated. Yes, a few parents complained about overbearing grandparents, but the real unhappiness came from those families whose grandparents were not interested in the new baby. I hope any grandparent who reads their words will make a special effort to fully share with the new parents the joy and excitement a baby brings. To miss out is a terrible loss for everyone.

You'll need no book to experience the deep thrill of that first grandchild, and just like first-time parents, you'll quickly find your own way to connect with and love that sweet baby. But I hope having some of this information in an easy-to-use reference will answer some of your questions and add to the fun ahead.

Most of all, I wish you the same great love and happiness my family has reaped from the first child of our new generation.

part I

Becoming a Grandparent

So You Are Expecting a Grandchild

"I just wanted the world to know I just became a grand-mother. What a thrill."

—SEEN POSTED ON THE INTERNET

My butcher has a sign on the wall reading, "Ask me about my grandson."

The best-dressed woman I know now spends most of her shopping time in the baby department.

When my most sophisticated friends get together, the first thing they do is swap baby pictures.

The tunes I find myself humming come from a CD called *Singable Songs for the Very Young*.

All of us are among the smitten. We are first-time grand-parents. If you are about to join the club, congratulations. Whether you've been waiting impatiently or the news was completely unexpected, the announcement that a first grand-child is on the way is very big news. It marks a major shift in

3

family roles—and the start of one of life's most wonderful and rewarding relationships. You're about to discover why the doting grandparents you know are so gaga over their grandchildren . . . why they carry those silly pictures around and actually look forward to baby-sitting . . . why one grandparent calls her grandchildren "my reward for the trials of raising children" and a cynical grandfather says, "Being a grandparent is the only thing I know that isn't overrated."

The bonding between grandparent and new baby is often instant, and the love so strong it takes many grandparents by surprise. Lots of grandparents say they are "in love" with their grandchildren. In fact, Dr. Arthur Kornhaber, a clinician who has studied the grandparent-grandchild bond, calls it the "most basic, purest form of human love, an unconditional love that is rooted deeply in the human spirit."

And oh, what fun lies ahead. You'll have the chance to repeat the best parts of parenthood—the joy and wonder of watching a unique human being develop—with none of the responsibilities. You won't have to worry about discipline or wake up for middle-of-the-night feedings. Your hopes and dreams won't be tied up with these children as they may have been with your own sons and daughters, so you can relax and simply enjoy them. Your only job is to love your grandkids and to be their special friend.

It's an exciting time to be a grandparent. For one thing, there are so many of us. It is predicted that by the year 2000 there will be 90 million grandparents, fueled by the "baby boomers" who began turning 50 in 1996.

Most of us are a new breed. We don't look like the stereotypical white-haired, stay-at-home rocking-chair grandmas and grandpas of the past. We are better educated, more youthful and energetic. And better able to take an active role in our grandchild's life. Grandparent-grandchild vacations, for example, are one of the fastest growing segments of the travel industry.

But long before these children are ready for travel adventures, we have a lot to offer them, and our role has never been more important. Chances are that your children are entering parenthood with a much more complicated life than when you became a parent. Two-income families are now the norm, and many very young children spend more time in day care than at home. Single parents are common. With less time with parents, children with nearby grandparents are doubly lucky. Babies need grown-ups who love them madly, who will spend one-on-one time with them, and grandparents fit the bill. You can do a lot to let a little one know that he or she is someone very special, and your own life will be all the richer for the experience.

Grandchildren can also create a special bridge between you and your adult children. Few events can so vividly underscore the true depth of family ties or strengthen bonds between parent and child than the start of a new generation. Suddenly, you have much more in common. Chances are one of your first reactions to learning a baby is on the way is to haul out the family albums, and take a trip down memory lane together. One grandmother reports that her first clue of changes to come was finding that her son, who always groaned at the sight of baby pictures, was suddenly as eager to see those pictures as she was.

I never knew how closely I was linked to my own daughter until she called at 3 a.m. to announce she was leaving for the hospital and found me, inexplicably, already wide awake!

Once the baby is born, you may find that your children see you in a different way and gain new appreciation of the challenges of parenting. "I feel a lot closer to my mother," a Pennsylvania mother says. "Becoming a mother myself has cemented the transition from mother-daughter to one of deep friendship as equals. It has been a very positive change." One New York grandmother was touched to have her daughter write a card for her birthday saying, "I never realized all you went through to bring me up."

Does becoming a grandparent mean you are getting old? On the contrary, the best part of seeing the world through the eyes of a brand-new human being is that it keeps us young! You can be a kid again, play games, sing songs, go to the zoo, get down on the floor and build a block tower, appreciate the wonder of the clouds and the flowers as you see them anew through the eyes of a young child. Little ones love to laugh, and they can bring out the happy, silly side of you that may have been put aside over the years.

Most of being a good grandparent comes naturally, so why a book for new grandparents? Because people who haven't been around babies for two or three decades will see a lot of changes and probably have a lot of questions. The rules of pregnancy are different today, and you may need assistance in understanding all the new terms surrounding pregnancy and a new baby, from amniocentesis to diaper genie to lactation consultant.

Some of the changes are purely practical—disposable diapers, more intelligent baby equipment. Others are more profound—many fathers are far more involved in the birth and the care of their children today. As happens with every generation, theories of infant care and child rearing have changed. Parents, who tend to be older today, are very serious about wanting the best for their babies, and even working mothers are willing to work at breast-feeding and to prepare baby food from scratch to insure that their little ones are off to a healthy start.

Grandparents who are not prepared for what is ahead aren't as supportive as they could be with a little more knowledge of what to expect. The pages ahead will answer some of the questions you may have, help you know what to anticipate when your children are expecting, and after the baby is born, as well.

Since shopping is one of the first and greatest pleasures for most grandparents, you'll find a guide to gifts large and small and find out what is worth buying for your own home.

If you haven't been around babies for two or three decades, you've probably forgotten a lot. When can you expect the baby to get his first tooth? To roll over, sit up, or crawl? What games can you play with a four-month-old? What should you read to a nine-month-old? When can the baby roll the ball back? Play peekaboo? What's a good lullaby besides "Rock-a-bye-baby"? What are the best toys for a two-year-old? Several chapters ahead is a brief refresher course to remind you of the basics of child development through the toddler years, and to help you make the most of your time with that wonderful baby.

Grandparents also may have issues to deal with such as divorce that were much less common when your children were born. Some of today's babies may have as many as eight grandparents and stepgrandparents. One chapter looks into these sometimes overextended families and how they are coping.

Some things do not change, of course. The tensions between parents and adult children don't disappear miraculously when a grandchild is born, and there's still the temptation to sometimes think you know better than your child what's best for the new baby. The often thorny question of getting along with in-laws remains, along with the dilemma of how to play a meaningful role in the life of a young grandchild who lives far away. Dozens of families have shared their experiences to help new grandparents negotiate these tricky areas. The names of contributors have not been used so that they could speak openly and honestly without fear of hurting anyone's feelings.

As with all human relationships, grandparenting will have its challenges, but they pale compared to the great joys ahead. Children with close, loving grandparents are lucky—but their grandparents are the luckiest of all.

What Will You Be Called?

Nanny or Granny? Grandpa or Poppy? Ginger and George? If you're like most of the families surveyed, you'll be plain old Grandma and Grandpa, but little ones who can't quite manage to pronounce these names properly have come up with dozens of original variations—

Grammy and Papa, Ma-maw and Paw-paw, Mi-mi, Ni-ni, Pop-pop, Bop-pop, Boo-mama, Bump-pa, and Bim-ma, to name a few. I've been christened "Gim-maw." One grandpa who has been dubbed "Gakki" says he would have it no other way—"I love being the only Gak on the block."

In the south, some families still use Big Mama and Big Daddy; other families teach traditional old-country names like Bubbie and Zaydie for Jewish children, Oma and Omo in German families, and Grandmere and Grandpere for the French. Nana, one of the most popular British names for grandmother, has the advantage of being one of the easiest names to say.

Sometimes maternal and paternal grandparents are told apart by using first names like Grandma Ruth and Grandpa Sam. One young grandmother named Wendy who didn't like the idea of being a granny came up with Mama Wen. Some grandparents simply prefer being called by their first names. This is especially useful in stepfamilies where Grandma and Grandpa are reserved for the natural grandparents.

So Your Child Is Expecting a Child

"I feel like a stereotype, but I love every minute."

Remember the days when the doctor scolded if a mother-to-be gained over 15 pounds? When mothers were sedated during the birth of their children and fathers first saw their babies through the glass wall of the nursery?

Get ready for some major changes, for pregnancy and childbirth for your children will likely be a decidedly different experience from what you recall. Prenatal testing that is now routine didn't even exist a few decades ago, and the rules for expectant mothers are a lot more relaxed. The hospital experience is often totally altered from what grandparents knew. All of these matters may leave many grandparents curious or puzzled. Here are answers to some of the queries, major and minor, that many grandparents have expressed.

- **Mothers-to-be today are allowed to gain much more weight during pregnancy than in the past. Why is this?**

Not to worry when you see your pregnant daughter or daughter-in-law putting on what seems an inordinate amount of weight. Doctors now say it was a mistake to limit weight gain as was done in the past, that the added pounds mean better nutrition for the baby. One of the old fears was that added weight increased the possibility of toxemia (a serious disease with symptoms that include edema or swelling and extremely high blood pressure), according to Dr. Bruce Young, Silverman Professor of Obstetrics and Gynecology and Director of Obstetrics at the New York University Medical Center. "We know now that this is not true," says Dr. Young, who is also Director of the Division of Maternal and Fetal Medicine at New York University.

Depending on the size of the mother, 25 to 35 pounds is now considered a healthy weight gain. Most of this gain disappears at birth. A seven-pound baby, plus a one-pound placenta and about 15 pounds of fluids adds up to 23 pounds. And now that babies are allowed to reach their full natural weight, as opposed to the past when weight was restricted, it is not unusual to have newborns weighing eight to ten pounds.

Any extra weight gained by the mother seems to disappear with no more effort than before. "My mother positively panicked when she heard I had gained 40 pounds," one young mother reports. "She was sure I would be a blimp forever. But six months later, I was thinner than when I started and I hadn't even tried very hard. When people asked how I did it, I laughed and said I was lifting weights—meaning my big, beautiful baby boy."

• **My daughter's friends are having her baby shower in the evening, with husbands included. Ours were always female-only affairs. Is this something new?**

Showers are still often held for women friends and relatives, but there is a growing trend toward picnics, brunches, or potluck suppers for couples, so that dads and granddads can share the fun. These male/female get-togethers are a reflection of the growing role of fathers.

Friends and siblings of the parents-to-be often host the shower, but parents can also fill this role. It may be a great way to endear yourself to a daughter-in-law. Just be sure to find out whether they prefer a coed party, and get a guest list from the parents-to-be so that you don't leave out anyone important.

• **My daughter was given a "diaper genie" at her shower. What on earth is that?**

The diaper genie is not a robot for changing the baby, but a contraption that compacts disposable diapers. Some parents love them; others say they are a waste of money because they never work right.

• **My daughter-in-law is in her eighth month of pregnancy and she is still taking aerobics classes. Can this really be healthy?**

Mothers-to-be are encouraged to continue with aerobics or enroll in classes of calisthenics specially designed for pregnancy. Those who regularly play tennis or any other sport are encouraged to continue. As long as things are proceeding well, moderate exercise not only gives a sense of well-being and improves circulation during pregnancy, but leaves the mother in better physical shape after the birth.

- **What exactly is a sonogram?**

A sonogram is a black-and-white image of the fetus in the womb created by ultrasound. It is produced by sound waves from an instrument moved around on the mother's abdomen and transmitted to a video monitor. This is a test done for almost all mothers-to-be, usually between the 16th and 18th week of pregnancy. It is used to accurately calculate the age and condition of the fetus, to try to pinpoint the probable due date, to detect multiple fetuses, and to pick up any serious visible abnormalities.

If you are invited, by all means go along for the sonogram. It is a unique opportunity and a thrill to "see" the baby inside the mother—at least to see the curve of the spine and the outlines of head, arms, and legs.

The trained eye of a doctor can also often detect the sex of the baby. It is up to the parents whether they want to know this in advance. But the prediction from this shadowy fetal picture is not infallible, so hold off on buying those pink or blue booties. Three families interviewed for this book discovered that technology hasn't yet done away with all the surprises of childbirth.

More serious is the fact that in rare cases sonogram diagnoses can be wrong, predicting what looks like an abnormality when one does not exist or missing a serious problem, either way causing enormous distress to the prospective parents and their families. The procedure is not perfect, but it is most often accurate and does often serve an important purpose.

• What is amniocentesis?

This advance in medical diagnosis is so called because it involves the cells and chemicals in the amniotic fluid surrounding the fetus. The test is usually given to mothers who are over 35 or have a history of gene-linked diseases or other problems, or those whose earlier test results were abnormal. A small sample of fluid is taken by passing a long, ultrathin needle through the abdomen and into the amniotic sac. Ultrasound is used before and during the procedure to guide the needle so that the fetus and placenta are avoided. By analyzing this fluid, doctors can detect neural defects, Down syndrome, and other genetic disorders. This is also another opportunity to determine the sex of the baby if the parents want to know.

• What is a "triple screen"?

A common blood test given to expectant mothers, usually between weeks 15 to 20, it is used to measure three substances produced by the fetus and placenta: alpha-fetoprotein (AFP), human choirionic conadotropin (hCG), and estriol. High or low levels of these substances can suggest neural-tube and other structural defects and genetic disorders such as Down syndrome. Ultrasound and amniocentesis are then used to give a more complete diagnosis.

• **I seem to hear of so many babies being born by cesarean delivery. Has the rate actually gone up?**

Indeed, the incidence of the procedure commonly known as a "C-section" has increased dramatically. In 1960, the odds were one in 20; today one out of four births are by cesarean, and in high-risk categories, the ratio goes up to one in three.

There are many reasons for this change. The trend toward higher weight gain means larger babies that are more difficult to deliver vaginally. There are many more older mothers with increased risk of problems during prolonged labor, and many more multiple births due to the use of fertility drugs.

Also, breach babies were delivered vaginally 25 years ago and that is seldom done today. Forceps deliveries, once so common, are rarely performed because of possible adverse effects on the baby.

The fact that problems during delivery often result in malpractice suits today has produced a more aggressive attitude on behalf of the baby, according to Dr. Bruce Young. "We've gotten so much better in the care of the mother that the focus has moved to the infant," he notes. "Fetal heart rate monitoring and the measurement of fetal distress enables doctors to know with far more accuracy how the baby is tolerating labor. If there is a reasonable probability of a problem, the doctor will often perform a cesarean to be safe. Protecting the baby is the prime concern."

The procedure itself has been improved, and mothers are usually able to have a local anesthetic, called an epidural, and be awake to see the birth of their babies. Nor does one cesarean delivery automatically rule out the possibility of a vaginal delivery the next time around. The circumstances of each birth are different.

Recognizing that this type of surgery may have been over-performed in recent years, the current trend is to hold down the number of C-sections. One of the criteria many women use in judging a hospital is a low rate of cesarean deliveries.

• What is a birthing center?

More and more, having a baby is being treated as a natural part of life rather than a medical event, something all members of the family should be able to share. Hundreds of hospitals across the U.S. have built new family-friendly maternity wings with "birthing rooms" that look more like a hotel suite than a hospital room. Rather than moving from place to place, the mother stays in this room, known as the LDR (Labor, Delivery, Recovery) or in some cases LDRP (Labor, Delivery, Recovery, Postpartum) room, and the staff makes the adjustments, wheeling in and out the necessary equipment.

This is a much warmer setting than the labor and operating rooms of the past, and allows for family members to be together. Often the mother is assigned one specially trained nurse, who oversees her care throughout labor. In some cases the same nurse has been trained to continue care after the birth, teaching the new mother how to breast-feed and bathe the newborn baby.

Some hospitals now have midwives on staff for mothers who prefer this more personal approach to childbirth without a doctor. Being able to have the birth in the hospital is very reassuring to both parents and worried grandparents, since medical personnel and necessary equipment are at hand should they be needed.

After birth, the baby is not put into a nursery, but moves in with the mother (rooming in). In progressive hospitals such as the Hennepin County Medical Center in Minneapolis, there are double beds so that the father can stay overnight, as well. Other hospitals provide sofa beds. All birthing rooms are furnished with rocking chairs and cradles. The well-equipped birth center that opened in 1996 at St. Luke's Roosevelt Hospital Center in New York offers the comforts of a whirlpool bath with each room, as well as a kitchen, TV, and VCR. Harris Methodist Hospital in Fort Worth, Texas, even provides a play area for young children.

- **My daughter showed me pictures in a book of positions for labor that are nothing like the old procedures. What is going on?**

The new approach is to let the mother find the most comfortable position, whether that means standing, leaning back, squatting, or in some cases even relaxing in a water bath. Many hospitals now provide warm-water baths in their birthing rooms. Natural childbirth without anesthetic or painkillers is encouraged wherever possible.

- **What is a birth plan?**

A number of progressive hospitals will allow the mother to prepare a birth plan with her wishes stated in advance, which can include refusing to have pain medication or an epidural to numb the birth area.

• What is a lactation consultant?

This is a relatively new profession of people specially trained to help mothers breast-feed successfully. Practitioners must pass certification exams, and many belong to an international association for lactation specialists to keep up-to-date on the field.

"People assume that breast-feeding is a natural thing that will come easily, but this is not so," says Yaffa Stark, a lactation specialist who works with new mothers at Kaiser Permanente hospitals in Los Angeles and follows up with telephone calls after they go home. "Many parents have difficulty getting started, and they are very unhappy because they feel they are failing their babies. And the problem is compounded by nonsupportive parents who don't understand why the mother doesn't just give the baby a bottle. I recommend that parents read up on the benefits and importance of breast-feeding before the birth of the baby, so that they can give the new mother the moral support she so badly needs."

• Will I be allowed to be present during the mother's labor or delivery?

Depending on where you live, it is very likely. As long as the birth appears to be normal and low-risk, in many cases grandparents are invited to take part. Rather than pacing the floor of a waiting room, fathers often act as active coaches for their wives during labor, and parents or siblings can be on hand to offer moral support.

A California grandmother spoke of the good feeling that she was helping her daughter and son-in-law by being present during labor. "Time goes slowly and conversation doesn't flow easily during the early stages of labor," she says. "We talked about it in advance, picked out a book, and I read aloud. It was calming and relaxing for everyone."

In another family, the grandmother-to-be spelled her son-in-law briefly so that he could take a break and get something to eat, which was greatly appreciated by both parents. Another family reported that the wife's sister had served this function.

But even if you are allowed to be present during labor, whether you should actually do so is a very personal matter that should be discussed beforehand with the prospective parents. I was surprised to be told at the hospital that I could stay with my daughter until she was actually delivering the baby. I remained with her for a while and then left when she went into advanced labor, fearing that she and her husband would feel that I was intruding on their special moments. I wished we had discussed this beforehand so I could have known her wishes.

Many expectant mothers prefer that only their husbands be present during the latter part of labor or the delivery, finding this a very personal moment. "My mother is a smotherer," one new mother says, "and I hate to be smothered. I love her, but I really didn't want her there."

I know of one New York family where a permanent rift was created when a mother-in-law came uninvited into the labor room during what the mother felt should be a private experience. "Though I've tried, I've never been able to totally forgive her," the mother says. "I thought it was the pushiest, most insensitive thing she could have done."

Several other mothers expressed displeasure about grandparents who asked to be present without being invited. One mother reluctantly agreed when her mother-in-law wanted to be in the delivery room, but became angry when she requested that the father-in-law be there, as well. "I felt she was overstepping her place," she explains. Another young woman was furious when her father kept insisting that they videotape the birth. "When I told him we would be too busy, he said he would do it. I said, 'No way.' "

Most parents can understand a mother's feelings about privacy. "When my daughter-in-law was in labor, I visited part of the time and spent the rest of the time in the waiting room with her parents," a North Carolina grandmother recalls. "I am a shy person myself, so I understood perfectly when she said she wasn't up to having visitors."

Grandparents, too, may be shy or reluctant to see their child in pain or experience the bloody reality of birth. "I was present, but I asked for a curtain to give the mother privacy," says one grandmother. "I loved seeing the baby right after his birth, but I just didn't know if I could stand seeing my daughter go through it."

However, grandparents who are invited and who want to be present for the birth of their grandchildren report being thrilled by the experience. "I was amazed my daughter would want us," one Kentucky grandmother reports. "I can't imagine doing that myself. But it was magical. My husband stayed up near my daughter's head, but I was right there behind the doctor. I saw the head, the eyes, nose, and mouth come out and I just went to pieces. I sobbed and sobbed. I was watching a miracle. Then they told us it was a girl; the parents had been told it would be a boy. It was all so exciting. Within five minutes all four of us had held her and she was 'our baby.' And she has been ever since; there is a special bond between us."

They're Going to Name Her *What*?

Are you ready for a Taylor or a Tyler? Popular baby names change with the times; if your children go along with current trends, here are some of the names you may expect, according to a mid-1990s top ten. Girls: Amanda, Ashley, Emily, Jennifer, Jessica, Nicole, Samantha, Sarah, Stephanie, Taylor. Boys: Andrew, Christopher, Daniel, David, Jacob, Joshua, Matthew, Michael, Nicholas, Tyler.

Where you live may change some of the names on the hit parade. Among girls in Texas, for example, Brittany and Victoria made the top-ten list. In New York, Tiffany, Michelle, and Daniele were among the winners; Jasmine was a favorite in San Francisco and Kayla in Florida. As for the boys, New Yorkers liked Brandon, San Franciscans added Alexander and Kevin, Texans took to John, and Floridians favored Austin.

One interesting trend is that several old-fashioned names that were in the top 50 in 1900 are on the upswing again among today's parents. Among them are Alice,

Amelia, Anna, Charlotte, Emma, Lillie, Maud, Rose, and Sophia for girls; Abraham, Benjamin, Charles, Henry, Isaac, and Samuel for boys. And England's young Prince Harry has helped to make the name popular once again. Won't Uncle Harry be pleased!

The New Baby

"I was only 41 when my grandson was born, and not too thrilled at the prospect of being a grandparent, so I didn't expect the overwhelming emotion on seeing my grandson. He's two now, and even today, when that little boy reaches out and puts his arms around me, there is no feeling to compare it to."

Few experiences in life can match the joyful emotion of watching your "baby" holding his or her own baby. Whether you've been present for the delivery or not, grandparents agree that the sooner you can see, hold, and welcome the new baby, the stronger the bonding. "There's something about being part of the miracle of creation," one grandparent explains. "I feel as though somehow I'll be closer to this baby forever because I knew him from the very start."

For grandparents who have forgotten how a newborn looks, especially grandmothers who were not awake for the birth of their own children, the first sight of a brand-new infant may be a surprise. Lots of newborns are wrinkled, scrawny creatures when they first arrive, with odd-shaped heads from being squeezed through the birth canal. When they first emerge they are purple until they get oxygen into their lungs, and their eyes may be puffy from drops applied to protect from infection. That doesn't stop either grandparents or parents from falling totally in love with their progeny. For those who are lucky enough to be present, the brand-new baby in its first moments with its mother and father is a sight that brings tears and deep emotions of joy that are never forgotten.

New parents agree that having their own thrilled parents present makes the birth a more joyful experience. If you can't be there in person, do all you can to express your love, they urge. Call often, and send something more personal than flowers.

"I really wanted my own mother when the baby was born," says one young woman, "but she lives far away and the baby came early, so there was no way. But she still managed to be part of things. She express-mailed a new robe and perfume for me and an outfit for the baby to wear home. I was really touched."

If you are on hand right after the birth, you'll hear another term that may be new to you: *the Apgar score.* This a test that is given one minute and again at five minutes after birth to measure the infant's condition. It was named for Dr. Virginia Apgar, who developed the test to allow medical personnel to quickly evaluate the state of a newborn, spotting those babies that need extra care. Her name neatly covers the vital signs nurses or doctors look for: **A**ppearance (skin tone), **P**ulse (the heartbeat), **G**rimace (reflex), **A**ctivity (muscle tone), and **R**espiration (breathing). A score of seven or above means the infant's outlook is bright; below seven calls for extra procedures, such as suctioning the air passages or administering oxygen.

If you're going to help take care of the baby and you need a refresher course, being around during the hospital stay can be beneficial. If your grandchild is born in a hospital where the baby stays with the mother, you can watch while the nurse teaches the new mom how to diaper and feed the baby. Even in more traditional settings, most hospitals welcome grandmothers in their sessions for new mothers, showing how to bathe an infant and how to swaddle the baby, snugly wrapping the little one in a receiving blanket, which is done for the first couple weeks of life, helping him to feel warm and secure.

With all the attention to the baby, don't forget that the new mother needs her share of tender, loving care. She's happy, but she's probably also stiff, sore, tired, and achy. While it may promote bonding, having the baby in the room means there's not much rest in the hospital. Soothing gifts like cologne, a massaging device, or a new loose-fitting outfit that is *not* a maternity dress will help to cheer her.

GOING HOME

In most cases, only a 48-hour stay is allowed after a normal birth, so mother and dad are quickly plunged into full-time responsibility for the baby, a prospect as scary as it is exciting. Nervous parents, weary from middle-of-the-night feedings, are adjusting to a new personality in the house; learning to hold, feed, and bathe the baby; and struggling to decipher what this tiny newcomer is trying to tell them when she complains. Is she getting too much or too little to eat? Does she need changing? Should she be picked up or allowed to cry? Will that colicky baby ever stop crying? The first weeks of a baby's life are a learning and testing period for all the family.

Should you move in for the first week or two to help? In most families this is a role filled by the grandmother, and whether she will be a help or a hindrance varies with the personality of the mother and her relationship with the parents. If being together causes tension, everyone might be better off if you pay for, or contribute to, hiring outside help. And some parents just don't want anyone else around the first week or two—they prefer to have the baby and the house to themselves. The solution to this first important issue should be guided by what the parents want, not based on your expectations.

If you are invited to stay and you feel comfortable, you can certainly help in a dozen ways—buy the groceries, cook dinner, do the laundry, clean the house, or watch the baby between feedings so the parents can take a nap. If you live nearby, you can help with much of this without moving in.

Don't overdo the bustle. Heed the words of the new mother who commented on her mother's stay, "We were glad that she was there, but we were glad when she left. She was great about doing laundry and cleaning, but because she was so busy all the time, she created a lot of motion. It was too much activity. I think she stressed out my husband a bit. They have a great relationship, but he couldn't really relax."

Be prepared to wait your turn with the baby. Much as you long to hold her and feed her, at the start the mother and father probably want to tend to their new baby themselves. And if the mother is nursing, no one else can help with feedings.

ABOUT NURSING

Establishing a successful nursing pattern is one of the first challenges facing new mothers. Breast-feeding was an option many grandmothers did not choose, but nursing today has become a badge of being a "good mother," and it is important for grandparents to understand why so they can be supportive. Sure, your children may have done just fine on formula, but breast-feeding offers many important advantages.

Human breast milk contains ingredients not found in cow's milk or formula. According to doctors, it is more digestible, less likely to cause overweight, rarely causes allergies, and babies who are breast-fed are often less subject to illness and have fewer ear infections in the first year, thanks to the transfer of immune factors in the mother's milk. More good reasons: nursing is economical, helps speed the shrinking of the uterus, and can help burn off the fat accumulated during pregnancy.

Add to this the emotional gratification, the intimacy, and sharing of love and pleasure between mother and child, and it becomes easy to understand why most mothers are determined to succeed.

Many mothers who go back to work even take time out during the day to express milk into bottles so that the baby will not need formula in the first months. Companies such as Cigma, a life and health insurance provider, and Bankers Trust, a New York bank, understanding how important this is to the mothers, have set up lactation centers in their offices equipped with hospital-grade breast pumps and washing facilities. They find that it pays to encourage mothers to breast-feed because their babies have fewer illnesses, meaning that mothers have fewer absences from work. Some even provide counseling from lactation consultants, who visit mothers during their maternity leave and help them plan their return to the office. They explain that it is good for morale and makes new mothers more comfortable about returning to their jobs.

However, the first few weeks of breast-feeding are difficult. It takes at least a month to establish a successful pattern. These are weeks fraught with worry for the mother over whether the baby is getting enough nourishment, plus concern that she is not a proper mother because something that seems so basic is not going well. Grandparents who have raised children on bottles are not always properly sympathetic during this period. One young mother reports worrying terribly over why the baby would only drink from one breast. "Instead of giving me moral support and helping me figure out why, my mom urged me to forget the whole thing."

Another mother, upset because her son was losing weight, recalls, "My father made me cry. He said I was starving the baby, that if I used a bottle, at least I would know how much milk he was getting."

"Of all the problems I or any of my new-mom friends encountered, this was the biggest," agrees an Indiana mother.

"None of our moms supported our feeding choice. I had some normal difficulties in the first two weeks. And every time my son would cry, my mom would be Johnny-on-the-spot with a bottle of formula. As appreciative as I was for her help, I was grateful when she left so that my son could establish a milk supply. Recently, he decided to wean himself. My mom's first comment was, 'Well, at least you're over *that* stuff.' "

On the other hand, mothers who decide to use a bottle may also need your support if they feel pressure to go along with the strong nursing trend.

MORE CHANGES

Respecting the mother's choices when it comes to caring for the baby has always been the most elemental rule of good grandparenting, but it is even more important today because so many mothers are a little bit older and a lot more serious about doing everything right for their children, as dictated by the latest studies and information from child-care experts.

You're likely to see many practices that are different from what you knew. Babies aren't placed on their tummies to sleep anymore; new thinking says this may promote crib death. When my grandchild was born in 1994, sleeping on the side was in vogue for infants; special bolsters were designed to keep the baby in the right position. Recently, I read that side sleeping is now "out"—sleeping on the back is the new preferred position. The answer is probably that healthy babies thrive whatever way they sleep, but like many facets of child care, each generation feels that their way is the better way, and each set of parents wants to keep up with the latest findings.

When babies are fed with a bottle, you may be shocked to see that there's no more sterilizing. While many doctors do still advise using the old methods, others say that if the water supply is safe and clean, there is no need to boil bottles and nipples, especially if the family has a dishwasher that allows water to reach high temperatures. Some doctors also say that if *you* can drink the water safely, you don't have to boil it before adding it to formula.

Don't be surprised if the baby is given the bottle cold. Some babies will take the bottle straight from the refrigerator happily, and it's undeniably a lot easier on the nerves than trying to warm the formula when the baby is screaming. Many experts say it's perfectly O.K. to give cold milk.

Most grandparents did not hesitate to feed their babies commercial baby food, but lots of mothers concerned with keeping sugar and additives out of their baby's lives buy food processors and puree their own fruits and vegetables for the baby, using an ice tray to freeze the food into single-serving cubes. Except for sleeping garments that must be made of fire-resistant synthetics, many mothers want only natural fibers and buy only all-cotton clothing for their little ones.

Even the sweet-smelling baby powder we sprinkled so lavishly on baby's bottom is out of favor. "(Powders) serve no medical purpose, can cause irritation if they collect in baby's cracks and crevices, can be dangerous if inhaled, and if they contain talc, may even cause lung cancer down the road," according to *What to Expect the First Year*, a popular current guide for parents. It makes you wonder how your family ever survived at all!

Occasionally traditional wisdom does win out. *The New York Times* reported that a compact disc, *Grandma's Colic Cure*, was created after Hope Clapp, a grandmother in Virginia, advised her granddaughter, Lisa Von Canon, to run the vacuum cleaner or clothes dryer to soothe her colicky infant son. The sound of this "white noise" worked so well that Lisa passed the advice on to her sister, Andrea Edmunds, who had similar success. Mrs. Edmunds's husband, Andy, a musician, then produced a CD of sounds from vacuum, hair dryer, clothes dryer, dishwasher, lawn mower, and water running into the tub. You'll find ordering instructions on page 175.

Right or wrong, you should not be surprised if your advice is ignored. Think back to how you bristled when your own parents talked about the "old days" or questioned how you did things. In every generation, grandparents who pooh-pooh new practices raise hackles. Just about every guide for new parents offers advice about how to handle unwelcome advice from grandparents.

When you get your chance to care for the baby, you'll definitely approve of some of the changes. Three cheers for Velcro—no more worry about sticking the baby with diaper pins or undoing knots in the strings of a bib. But you'll find it takes dexterity to master the sticky tabs on disposable diapers or the Velcro tabs on the wraparound rubber pants that hold on cloth diapers these days. Get a lot of practice while you have a placid infant so you'll be adept by the time you are dealing with a wriggling toddler.

As tiny and helpless as the baby may be, you'll soon see that he has a personality and a temperament all his own. As you once learned for yourself, some babies are easily soothed, others are not; some gulp their bottles or take breast milk eagerly, others have to be coaxed. Discovering the differences that already make this tiny baby different from all others is part of the wonder of grandparenting.

The Wonder of a New Grandchild

"Nothing prepared me for the rush of emotions, the urge to hold the baby, to connect, let him know he's a part of me and I'm a part of him, and that I'll always love him and be there for him."

"It goes beyond words. Holding a newborn is a wonderful experience—such innocence. Then we watched her get weighed and measured. She was left in the bassinet in the nursery for a few moments and cried hard. I wanted so much to pick her up and comfort her."

"When I saw my baby holding her baby, I felt like my heart was turning over inside me. I couldn't believe the strength of the emotion. I got all choked up and wept with joy."

"It was a tremendous, overwhelming rush of emotion, a beautiful, strange feeling that brought tears to my eyes. He was so perfect, so beautiful. I found myself thinking of my own parents, who are no longer living. I wished they could be here to witness my feelings. I wished I could speak to them to ask if they had felt the same."

"I was present during labor and delivery. I cried with joy. I couldn't believe how small he was and how perfectly formed. I couldn't believe that one minute he had been inside her and the next, there he was! It was a wonderful experience."

"I was overcome with emotion when I saw my newborn grandson. I thought of all the years when I had been too busy earning a living to spend time with my own son, his father. I vowed that I would not make the same mistake a second time."

"When they brought my grandson into the nursery, it felt like my world had come full circle. At that moment there was nothing more beautiful than that screaming little baby, a part of myself. Later I was allowed into the nursery and I went in alone to pick up my grandson for the first time. I wanted this moment to be only between him and me. I sat with him in a rocker with tears streaming down my face. One of the nurses looked at me and said, 'Isn't it beautiful to be a grandmother?' All I could do was nod."

"We were sitting in the waiting room and saw my daughter being wheeled by and she said, 'Dad, I will see you in a minute, I'll be right back.' And then she came back and we went to her room and saw the baby and I was speechless, crying, happy. My heart was beating 500 beats per minute, it seemed. When my first child was born, I was 22, and it seemed to be a normal thing that we took for granted. But watching my grandson, I thought, 'What a miracle.' "

Watching the Baby Grow

"I couldn't believe how much I had forgotten. I raised three kids, but each new thing the baby does is a thrill, as though I'd never seen anyone do this before."

The development of a tiny, helpless baby to a walking, talking toddler is a miraculous journey, and watching it unfold is one of the greatest joys of grandparenting.

Even as infants, babies are mastering particular developmental tasks. From her very first days, your grandchild is acquiring a basic outlook on life, developing trust that her needs will be met, that she will be fed when hungry, cuddled and loved, and given sensory and intellectual stimulation through play. Though parents play the starring role in supplying these needs, you can be an important member of the supporting cast. Talking and singing to her, holding and kissing her are your natural expressions of love, and each time you play with her you are teaching her valuable lessons. Babies learn to talk by being talked to, and they learn to love by being loved. Everything you say and do is being stored in her tiny brain, and helping to form her personality and her knowledge about the world as a loving place.

One of the most valuable things you can do is to read to your grandchild. Even the infant stage is not too soon to begin. The comfort of nestling together when you read and the sound of your voice are important elements in bonding between you and the baby, and she is absorbing more than you might think. I had no idea when I began reading to Jackson when he was an infant how much he understood. I was amazed to see that at six months he began to laugh aloud when I read him the happy ending of the book *The Carrot Seed*. He couldn't possibly have understood that a carrot seed had sprouted, but he *could* read the happiness in my voice and responded in kind. He loves that book to this day.

The tried-and-true first baby book is *Pat the Bunny*. Put her tiny finger on the page to feel the bunny's softness and the scratchiness of a daddy's beard. You can move on to some of the classic books for very young children, all now available in sturdy cardboard versions so that baby will be able to turn the pages herself as soon as she is a little older. You'll find a list of suggestions on page 171.

HOW DOES THE BABY GROW

Though children follow a general developmental timetable, no two children are alike, and they will master each skill when their muscles and minds are ready and not a minute before. Inexperienced, nervous parents worry when babies don't conform to charts, but if you've raised a child or two yourself, you should know better, even though you may be faced with "can you top this" tales of prodigy grandchildren from your friends.

There's a huge variation in "firsts," whether first tooth or first steps. By the time a child is school age, it makes no difference whether she was toilet trained at two or three, whether she walked earlier or later than the norm, or how many words she knew at 18 or 24 months.

However, it's human nature to want to know what to expect in the months ahead, especially for grandparents who have forgotten what happens when. One thing not to expect is a smooth journey through early childhood. The late Louise Bates Ames, a cofounder of the Gesell Institute of Human Development, found in extensive research that definite periods of what she calls "harmony and disharmony" alternate throughout childhood in a series of emotional spurts and setbacks for child and family alike. The most trying times come when the child is experiencing her own growing pains and frustrations. In the first year of life these ups and downs come as often as every four weeks; in the preschool years, about every six months. The good news in these findings is that you can relax through the fussy stages, knowing that sunnier days will soon follow.

THE FIRST SIX MONTHS

How helpless that little infant seems in the first weeks of life! She can't talk, can't even hold up her head. But in her own way, she is watching, listening, smelling, tasting, and absorbing the world around her. She cries for help, quiets when she is held or fed, learns to nestle her body against yours. She can't say it yet, but she is identifying the special people in her life and is learning how to love.

Along with connecting, part of her job in the first six months is to figure out that she is separate from those who take care of her and to develop independence. This struggle will continue in various ways until she is an adult.

ONE TO THREE MONTHS: ADAPTING TO THE WORLD

Independence for an infant begins with control over her own body, and by the second month she is already making some progress. She can hold her head up briefly, and she may even attempt to grab at something that attracts her. She has begun to exercise her arms and legs lying on her back, to look longer at objects.

Somewhere between 8 and 12 weeks comes one of the most rewarding moments of parenting—the first, real, unmistakable smile, and grandparents get their share of smiles, too. By her third month, the baby smiles often. She is no longer governed only by immediate physical needs. Her crying decreases, and she is responsive, gurgling and cooing in reply to sounds. She begins to recognize and differentiate family members. By now she has discovered her own hands and feet, examines them endlessly, and explores her own face and mouth with touch. She is equally interested in the faces of those who care for her. She is showing the first signs of memory, waiting for expected rewards like feedings. She is also moving more vigorously, flexing her little legs, beginning to lean on her elbows, and holding her head up for longer periods each week.

In the first three months, as vision is developing, the colors children see most clearly are black and white, so a first mobile in those colors makes a good gift. (See page 156 for more age-appropriate gifts.)

THREE TO FOUR MONTHS: GROWING AWARENESS

Around 14 weeks, most babies can follow a slowly moving object with eyes and head, and will stop sucking to listen to a sound and look for its source.

Though the world must still be brought to your little one, she is ready for more interaction with people and things. She wants to be talked to, played with, allowed to touch and feel different textures—a squashy beanbag, a hard rattle, a plush teddy bear, a rubber squeeze toy. A crib gym and floor gyms with toys that she can see, reach for, and eventually use actively are welcome playthings.

In the fourth month, as physical ability increases and movements take on determination, the baby becomes a show-off. Now she rolls to her side and may even start to roll from back to stomach—or vice versa. She laughs and splashes in the bath and kicks her legs on the diapering table, strengthening muscles for the work that lies ahead. Her eye/hand coordination is improving. By the end of this month, she will probably be seeing her surroundings in color and be able to focus well at different distances, though she will still prefer what is in front of her to what is across the room. Her moods show that she is increasingly delighted with what she can do.

FIVE TO SIX MONTHS: SITTING UP, STRANGER ANXIETY

Now her eyes begin to lead her hands and she will soon be reaching for objects with good aim, intent on touching, tasting, chewing, and manipulating anything in sight, an urge that will soon lead to the desire to move toward things. Her first progress may be by rocking, rolling, and twisting, and she may go backward or sideways at first, but she will be crawling forward in no time at all.

Somewhere around six months she will be able to sit up without support, a major milestone.

The many early unsuccessful efforts to sit, roll over, and crawl can lead to frustration, however. There are abrupt mood changes from sunny to sullen during this period, sometimes aggravated by teething pains. Better listen to the baby's mother on what to do to soothe teething pain. Old remedies like a drop of brandy on the gums may not be in tune with current thinking.

Somewhere between six and nine months, as baby becomes increasingly able to distinguish among the people around her, she may begin to exhibit what many researchers call "stranger anxiety." Now she will withdraw and show fear of people outside her home circle; she might even shrink from grandparents or other close relatives who are not daily visitors. This is a universal and temporary phase, so don't feel rejected.

During these shy periods, don't rush toward the baby. Let her size things up and make the first overtures herself.

By the end of six months individual differences in personality and physical ability become much clearer. One child might crawl forward eagerly, another might be more interested in making sounds, and a third might be busy with visual stimuli, studying the minute details of every object in her path. Each of these babies is behaving in a completely normal way.

SEVEN MONTHS: MIXED EMOTIONS

By her seventh month, your grandbaby may be crawling on her stomach and sitting for several minutes without support. Pretty soon she will be on her hands and knees as crawling goes into high gear—and you'll have to move fast to keep up. You can encourage crawling with games like rolling a ball and encouraging the baby to "go get it," or getting down on your own hands and knees to "chase" the baby.

Now's the time for a safety check of your home before she comes to visit; she wants to touch, toss, and taste everything she can reach. (See page 78 for information on baby-proofing your home.)

Her mind is also making giant strides. She can recall past events and anticipate the future. She imitates sounds as well as behavior, and loves games like "So Big," "Peekaboo," and "This Little Piggy." If you exercise her arms and legs while she is lying on her back, she may reward you with peals of laughter.

EIGHT TO NINE MONTHS: GETTING AROUND

Curiosity leads eight-month-olds to begin trying to pull up to a standing position, a process of trial and error that is fascinating to watch. By the end of the ninth month some children can stand without holding on to a support and may be starting the journey along table edges and sofas that leads to walking. A few children actually walk at nine or ten months, the majority around one year, other perfectly healthy and normal children not until 15 or 16 months.

Beginning around nine months you'll see a change in the baby's play. She still likes shaking and banging one-piece toys, but now likes to grasp a separate object in each hand and begins to stack and to put smaller objects into larger ones. This is a sign of growing dexterity and of learning important concepts. Stacking teaches spatial relationships; nesting is a way of experimenting with size differences, discovering what is larger and smaller. Filling and dumping is a favorite activity that you can provide for with toys as well as with all kinds of things around the house.

This is also the beginning of a phase when babies love to drop and throw things. Food and toys go off the feeding tray, stuffed animals go out of the crib. She isn't trying to annoy; she's actually practicing a new skill, being able to let go of things.

TEN MONTHS: FEELING FRICTION

Because a mobile baby encounters so many don'ts, she is often confused and frustrated and quick to voice her dismay. By ten months, there is definite friction between the baby and those who take care of her. She is torn between wanting to please and the need to discover things for herself. Caregivers find themselves in the unpleasant position of constantly saying no.

As compensation for the inevitable conflicts that mobility brings, there is the fun of watching your grandchild make leaps and bounds in social and intellectual growth. At ten months, she can understand some words and commands, and may repeat a few words over and over. She knows her name and will begin to imitate you when you say easy words like "hi," "bye-bye," and "uh-oh." If you open your arms, she'll come over.

Eleven Months to One Year: An Individual

By now children can participate actively in games like hide-and-seek, peekaboo, waving bye-bye. They love hiding behind a door or curtain and hearing you say, "Where's Janie?" and "There she is" when she peeks out.

By her first birthday, your baby is making clear her likes and dislikes. She is probably doing nicely with finger foods and learning to hold a spoon and drink from a cup, understands much that is said to her and may be babbling a few words. She is her own little person with a definite personality.

GAMES THAT BABIES LOVE

It's hard to say who has more fun playing games, Grandma and Grandpa or the baby. Traditional hand games like "Pat-a-Cake" and "So Big" are enjoyed even by tiny infants; they involve touch, gentle exercise, and your loving voice—all important steps in a baby's growth. Very soon, he will show you how much he likes to play by laughing when you go through these motions. In no time he will be doing the motions and saying words himself, because while you are having fun together you are teaching important lessons.

You probably remember many games, and new ones will come naturally as you play with the baby, but just to refresh your memory and extend your repertoire, here's a collection of games that grandparents and parents report their babies loved to play. (See page 184 for resources for music for sing-along games.)

Peekaboo

This is a favorite from baby days right through the toddler years. Hold a diaper or scarf or the corner of a blanket in front of your face and say, "Where's Grandpa?" Pull it away and say, "Here I am." As the baby gets older, you can cover his face lightly and say, "Where's Johnny?" Whisk it away and say, "*There* he is." Once Johnny is crawling, he'll do his own variations, hiding behind the door or the draperies.

Face Fun

Take baby's hand and move it around your face, saying hair, eyes, nose, mouth, ears; now do the same on baby's face. When she can point her finger, use the finger to touch each part. She'll soon be touching and saying the names herself.

Fingers and Toes

Take baby's index finger and touch each of the outstretched fingers on your other hand, saying, "Grandma has one, two, three, four, five fingers." Then use your index finger to hold up the baby's hand and touch her fingers, saying, "And Sarah has one, two, three, four, five fingers."

KIDDY CALISTHENICS

Babies enjoy being held upright and given help moving their arms and legs before they can stand or exercise for themselves. As soon as the baby can hold his head up firmly, you can stand him on your lap and bounce him gently or pull him to a sitting position or standing position.

When baby is on his back, you can put him through his paces. Move his arms above the head, then move them to the side, then across the chest, and up again, counting, "One, two, three, four. Do the motions once more." Then hold his feet and bend the legs up and down to the same count.

"Did You Ever See a Lassie"

Move the baby's hands back and forth in time to the music.
Did you ever see a lassie
A lassie, a lassie
Did you ever see a lassie
Go this way and that?
Go this way and that way
And this way and that way

Did you ever see a lassie
Go this way and that?

"I'm a Little Teapot"

This is one of the cutest games to watch baby learn to do on his own.
I'm a little teapot short and stout
Here is my handle (place baby's hand on hip so the elbow sticks out)
Here is my spout (turn the other hand out)
When I get all steamed up, hear me shout
Tip me over and pour me out (tilt the baby to the left).

MUSICAL EXERCISES
"Row, Row, Row Your Boat"

Push the feet in a pedaling motion, in time to the song.
Row, row, row your boat
Gently down the stream
Merrily, merrily, merrily, merrily
Life is but a dream.

"The Wheels on the Bus"

Move baby's arms to follow the verses.
The wheels on the bus go round and round, round and round, round and round
The wheels on the bus go round and round, all over town.

(Next verses:)
The people on the bus go up and down.
(arms up and down)
The wipers on the bus go swish, swish, swish.
(arms from side to side)
The horn on the bus goes beep, beep, beep.
(beep the belly button)
The ride on the bus goes bump, bump, bump.
(bounce the baby gently)

So Big, So Much

Ask, "How big is the baby?" Then pull his arms up high and say, "So big." "How much do I love the baby?" Pull his arms out wide and say, "So much."

CLAPPING GAMES

These can begin around four months and in a couple of months, baby will be able to bring his hands together himself.

Pat-a-Cake

The old game still delights a new generation.
Pat-a-cake, pat-a-cake, baker's man (clap the hands)
Bake me a cake as fast as you can (clap the hands)
Roll it and roll it and mark it with B (roll the hands)
And put it in the oven for baby and me. (Tuck the hands into baby's tummy.)

Clap Hands

Clap hands, clap hands 'til Daddy comes home
For Daddy has money and Mommy has none.
(. . . or the new politically correct version:)
Clap hands, clap hands 'til Mommy comes home

If You're Happy

As baby gets older, you can add to these verses—substitute any of these for clapping your hands: tap your head, wave your hand, stamp your feet, etc.
If you're happy and you know it, clap your hands
(clap, clap)
If you're happy and you know it, clap your hands
(clap, clap)
If you're happy and you know it, then clap your hands and show it
If you're happy and you know it, clap your hands (clap, clap).

Tickle Time

Tickle games will bring peals of laughter. Here's the classic, This Little Piggy, and a few alternates.

This Little Piggy

Touch the baby's toes one at a time working toward the pinkie
and at the last line run your fingers up the body.
This little piggy went to market
This little piggy stayed home
This little piggy had fine roast beef
This little piggy had none
And this little piggy cried, "Wee, wee, wee," all the way
home.

Buzzing Bees

Make a fist and say, "Here's the beehive, where are the bees?"
Open the fist and wiggle your fingers as they "fly" down to
tickle the baby while you go, "ZZZZ-ZZZZ-ZZZZ."

Eensy Weensy Spider

Use your index and third fingers to "walk" up the baby's body
slowly, then quickly run down again; pull his hands up high for
the sun, then run your fingers up again.
The eensy weensy spider went up the water spout
Down came the rain and washed the spider out
Out came the sun and dried up all the rain
And the eensy weensy spider went up the spout again.

Snail and Mouse

Walk your fingers up slowly, then down quickly as you say:
Slowly, slowly creeps the snail
Slowly up the garden rail
Quickly, quickly runs the mouse
Quickly, quickly round the house.

Hickory, Dickory

Hickory, dickory dock
The mouse ran up the clock (run fingers up)
The clock struck one (tap with one finger)
And down he run (run fingers down)
Hickery, dickery dock.

Tummy Time

Here are baby's fingers (touch fingers)
Here are baby's toes (touch toes)
Here is baby's belly button (touch it)
Round and round it goes (make circles on her tummy).

Knee Rides

Nursery rhymes provide the rhythm as you give baby a ride.
Here are some old-timers in case you've forgotten the words:

"Seesaw, Margery Daw"

Seesaw, Margery Daw
Jacky shall have a new master
Jacky shall have but a penny a day
Because he can work no faster.

"Jack and Jill"

Jack and Jill went up the hill
To fetch a pail of water
Jack fell down and broke his crown
And Jill came tumbling after.

"Humpty Dumpty"

Humpty Dumpty sat on a wall
Humpty Dumpty had a great fall
All the king's horses and all the king's men
Couldn't put Humpty together again.

"Little Miss Muffet"

Little Miss Muffet sat on a tuffet
Eating her curds and whey
There came a big spider who sat down beside her
And frightened Miss Muffet away.

"To Market, to Market"

To market, to market, to buy a fat pig
Home again, home again, jiggety jig
To market, to market, to buy a fat hog
Home again, home again, jiggety jog.

"Baa, Baa, Black Sheep"

Baa, baa, black sheep
Have you any wool?
Yes sir, yes sir, three bags full
One for the master and one for the dame
And one for the little boy who lives down the lane.

"Yankee Doodle"

Yankee Doodle came to London
Riding on a pony,
He stuck a feather in his cap
And called it macaroni.

"Wee Willie Winkie"

Wee Willie Winkie runs through the town
Upstairs and downstairs in his night gown
Rapping at the window, crying through the lock
Are all the children tucked in bed?
It's now eight o'clock.

"Old MacDonald"

Old MacDonald had a farm
E-I-E-I-O
And on his farm he had some chicks
E-I-E-I-O
With a peep, peep here and a peep, peep there
Here a peep, there a peep
Everywhere a peep, peep
Old MacDonald had a farm, E-I-E-I-O.
(Change the animal in next verses:)
Duck—quack, quack
Cow—moo, moo
Turkey—gobble, gobble
Pig—oink, oink
Donkey—hee-haw

"Dickery, Dickery Dare"

Dickery, dickery dare
The pig flew up in the air
The man in brown
Soon brought him down
Dickery, dickery dare.

"Horse Ride"

This is the way the ladies
ride, trot, trot, trot

This is the way the gentlemen
ride, canter, canter, canter
This is the way the farmers
ride, gallop, gallop, whee.

CIRCLE AND MOTION GAMES FOR TODDLERS

You probably remember these old-timers to be done walking in a circle, holding hands; little ones never tire of falling down at the end of the song.

"Ring Around the Rosy"

Ring around the rosy
A pocket full of posies
Upstairs, downstairs (alternative: ashes, ashes)
We all fall down.

"London Bridge"

London Bridge is falling down
Falling down, falling down
London Bridge is falling down
My Fair Lady.

Build it up with iron bars
Iron bars, iron bars
Build it up with iron bars
My Fair Lady.

"BINGO" (Stamp your feet in time to the letters.)

I know a man who had a dog
And Bingo was his name-o
B-I-N-G-O, B-I-N-G-O, B-I-N-G-O
And Bingo was his name-o.

Baby Lullabies

Of course, there's "Rock-a-Bye Baby," but what else can you sing to croon that little one to sleep? Here are some old favorites:

"All Through the Night"

Sleep, my child, and peace attend thee
All through the night
Guardian angels God will send thee
All through the night.
Soft and drowsy hours are creeping
Hill and vale in slumber sleeping
I, my loving vigil keeping,
All through the night.

"Sweet and Low"

Sweet and low, sweet and low
Wind of the western sea,

Low, low, breathe and blow,
Wind of the western sea.
Over the rolling waves we go,
Come from the dying moon and blow,
Blow him again to me;
While my little one, while my pretty one,
Sleeps.

"Hush Little Baby"

Hush little baby, don't say a word
Papa's gonna buy you a mockingbird
If that mockingbird don't sing
Papa's gonna buy you a diamond ring
If that diamond ring turns brass
Papa's gonna buy you a looking glass
If that looking glass gets broke
Papa's gonna buy you a billy goat
If that billy goat don't pull
Papa's gonna buy you a cart and bull
If that cart and bull turn over
Papa's gonna buy you a dog named Rover
If that dog named Rover don't bark
Papa's gonna buy you a horse and cart
If that horse and cart fall down
You'll still be the sweetest little baby in town.

"Sleep, Baby, Sleep"

Sleep, baby, sleep
Thy father tends the sheep
Thy mother shakes the dreamland tree
And downward comes a dream for thee,
Sleep, baby, sleep.

The Toddler Years:
One to Three

"It is wonderful for me to see my son's face light up when his grandparents come. It fills me with joy."

There is nothing cuter in the whole world than watching a toddler in action. This determined explorer on wobbly legs is nonstop motion, and with good reason. He is practicing, learning how to develop his large and small muscles in order to be more confident of his growing ability to walk—and eventually to run, climb, and jump.

Mobility marks a real change in children's behavior. Toddlers are so adorable and parents and grandparents long to show their affection, yet little ones at this stage may not want to be held or hugged. The days when the baby does just what you want are over, but the rewards are growing bigger. Soon you'll be able to really talk to your grandchild and to do so many things together.

You'll begin to see changes in your grandchild's physique

once he is walking. The pudgy baby fat will start to disappear between one and two, and by the time he is three, he will have the slim, limber frame of a preschooler.

As much as they long to be more independent, it's best to remember that toddlers are not as grown up as they would like to be. They can be unpredictable, liable to dart toward the street or climb where they don't belong. Keep a sharp eye out when you are in charge.

ONE TO TWO: ADORABLE REBELS
15 TO 21 MONTHS: FUSSY AND FRUSTRATED

Both locomotion and language grow by giant leaps in the second year of life, but this bounding baby is not always easy to live with. He will tend to say no before he says yes, to throw things before he becomes interested in picking them up, to run away before responding to an invitation to come near. Some people compare this period to the toddler being on a one-way street—usually leading in the opposite direction from the one grown-ups have in mind.

Delighted with his newfound walking ability, the one-and-a-half-year-old is motor-minded and moves ahead heedlessly until something gets in the way. That strong motor drive, the need to grab, and the lack of inhibition make the child of this age a small menace unless he is carefully watched.

With all the progress he has made, his abilities are still rudimentary, and life holds many unhappy surprises. He falls down when he wants to stay upright. Things drop when he wants to hold them. He lacks the words to express his very definite demands. He can't carry out his intentions, and he often takes out his frustration on the people caring for him. He is fussy about having his own way and grabby about possessions. Getting through daily routines is not easy. If Johnny does not want to have a new diaper, you'll have a tough time cajoling him to change his mind. Be sure to have plenty of distractions on hand—read a book, turn on a music box—anything to make him forget for the moment his determination to have his way.

Since the child's arms and hands still work better than his fingers, sand, clay, and water that can be scooped make great play materials during this period. But he is gaining more dexterity. Now your toddler can fit a round block into a round hole, make strokes with crayons on paper, and build a tower of three or four blocks—which he will probably promptly knock down. He can entertain himself for longer periods of time, can turn the pages of a book himself, put objects into and shake them out of a plastic milk bottle.

MOVING TOWARD TWO: LITTLE TALKERS

Language increases dramatically this year. On average at one year, children know perhaps a dozen or so words. By age two, some children have a vocabulary of 200 words. But they still know a lot more than they can express. When words fail little ones, gestures, sounds, pointing, and pulling will still make their wishes clearly known.

Saving Baby Talk

Can you remember all the adorable things your children said way back when? Lots of times these special sayings fade with time, but Anne Oakley, a grandmother in North Carolina, helped insure that her daughter, Margaret Buckner, will be able to pass on the memories to her daughter, Elizabeth. Anne suggested that her daughter keep a notebook-diary of the sayings, a record that Margaret says she already treasures. Some of her favorites: "Come in" for amen; "hiccup truck" for pickup truck; "ammuny," Elizabeth's first word for bunny (taken from the title of a book, *I Am a Bunny*); "Jesus in the badger" for Jesus in the manger.

If the parents aren't interested, keep your own notebook. Someday they'll be glad you did.

Somewhere around 18 months, the wave of opposition peaks in many children. As new abilities appear, their egocentricity shifts to outgoingness, ushering in a sunny transition period to age two. Depending on the maturity of the child, this may begin anytime between 18 and 21 months. Enjoy it, because this tranquil period will be followed by the infamous "terrible twos."

TWO TO THREE: CALM BEFORE THE STORM

This much-dreaded year is ushered in gently. Once again, children have become affectionate and agreeable, and life seems serene. Once more he is in love with his mommy and daddy, and happily receives his grandparents. He likes to run little errands, loves to go for walks, remembers where things belong—and likes to put them there. He enjoys working beside you and imitating what you do.

Language continues to grow. Single words expand to two- and three-word phrases and eventually to full sentences. Don't expect correct grammar. Words like "the" and "a" come last. He'll say, "Frow Gamma," instead of "I'm throwing to Grandma." Little girls generally seem to be more verbal, talking sooner and better than boys. Lots of children find it hard to say consonants correctly; this requires control over tongue and lip muscles that may not come until much later, and that may be just as well. "Baby talk" is so endearing, you may actually be disappointed when it disappears.

He still puts things in his mouth, but now he is more concerned with finding out what he can do with them. He feels, drops, and squeezes things to see what will happen. He is experimenting with being other people, as well, being a bus driver or trainman, for example. This is the age when children begin to love dressing up in your old clothing.

You may be shocked to find that your toddler grandchild can already count and identify letters. Does this mean you have a genius in the family? More likely it means he watches a lot of *Sesame Street,* where numbers and letters are repeated over and over, reinforced with colorful characters and catchy music. Some children are actually gaining pre-reading and pre-math skills from this; others are simply repeating what they see by rote without understanding the meaning. There's no harm done either way, and no question that *Sesame Street* and other educational TV shows have made a difference. Kindergarten curriculum is more advanced today because so many children come in with familiarity with their ABCs and numbers. But children who come to kindergarten with a head start don't necessarily stay ahead. Bright youngsters will quickly catch up.

When he comes to visit, your library can include fun number and letter books, but don't push or worry if he doesn't seem interested. Above all, be sure there are plenty of colorful storybooks, so he'll want to read with you and look forward to learning how to read on his own.

TWO-AND-A-HALF: STORM WARNINGS

The good days of the early twos are a temporary lull, leading up to more turbulent times when "no" will become his favorite word. How trying this "terrible twos" period will be depends on your grandchild's disposition. Johnny, who is easy to get along with, may simply turn a little bit fussy. Jason, a more difficult child, may mount a war of stubborn resistance. Not until the teen years will such moodiness and parental resistance surface again so strongly in many families. Some child development experts actually refer to this period as "first adolescence."

This is a time of self-centeredness, of bragging about independence with boasts like "I can take my *own* coat off." He doesn't want to be pushed in the stroller anymore—at least not until he is exhausted from running. He'll fight taking your hand to cross the street, though this is one issue that is not negotiable. One grandmother managed a compromise by having her grandson agree to let her hold the back of his collar while they crossed.

Your grandchild may sound like a little tyrant, bossing everyone around. Just remember that this bossiness is not because he is so sure of himself but just the opposite—the world seems big and frustrating, so having his way in even a small part of it is reassuring.

Most of the rebellion during the twos is directed against parents, so you may be particularly welcome as a baby-sitter during these periods when mother and father badly need a break.

When you are caring for your grandchild during the "no" stage, the easiest thing is to avoid confrontations. Try not to ask questions that can be answered with "no." Instead of saying, "Pick up your toys," say, "After the toys are put away we can go out to the park."

Too many choices are unwise, but giving simple choices may give the child a welcome feeling of control. Ask, "Do you want your lunch before or after we read your book?"

And you'll find that even the difficult two-and-a-half-year-old has his endearing moments. He is continuing to grow and learn. His coordination is better and his motor skills are increasing. He can work simple puzzles, is beginning to use paintbrushes and crayons more adeptly, and can play his own tape recorder. In his good moments, he can be lovable, engaging, and appreciative of everything and everybody around him.

THREE TO FOUR: WE VERSUS ME

By age three, tensions have eased and the welcome word "yes" reappears in the vocabulary, along with "we," as in "Can we play a game?" Feeling better about what he can do, the child seems able now to say "help me" or "show me" in order to learn more. He wants to cooperate, to do things right, to please you.

One reason he feels better about things is that he has much better control over his body, walking and running easily with fewer falls. His language skills have grown, allowing him to express what is on his mind.

Somewhere halfway through the third year there will be another curve in the spiral. Often when a developmental spurt occurs, inner security seems to dissolve and an outgoing, pleasant child may turn inward and stubborn. At three and a half, your grandchild may once again refuse to obey and constantly test his will against others. Bossiness returns as he orders, "Don't look," or "Don't talk." He wants his own way, wants to feel as big and capable as the grown-ups around him.

Insecure within yet determined to dominate, a child at this stage is filled with turbulent emotions, and his inner tensions show. He may suddenly burst out crying if things aren't going well. He gets frightened easily. Thumb-sucking, nail-biting, nose-picking, and other signs of stress may appear, and the security blanket can become a lifeline.

But not to worry—this is a temporary regression and these worrisome habits will disappear. Just as he seems most impossible, the stage will pass and he will suddenly turn loving and sunny once again.

Somewhere around age three, friends begin to be important, cooperative play first begins to appear, and he can truly enjoy the company of children his own age—and sometimes imaginary friends as well.

Toward the end of the third year, children reach the end of what is usually labeled the toddler years, moving on to the "preschool" stage. They are becoming more grown up, social and independent in many ways, and their world is widening. Now you can begin thinking about movies, outings, and some of the other treats you've been looking forward to sharing with your grandchild.

Shared Adventures

You don't have to spend a lot of money to plan toddler outings that will please both generations. Because grandparents are so eager to do special things with and for our grandchildren, we sometimes rush things. When he was one and a half, I took Jackson to the Central Park Zoo, only to discover I should have saved my money. He was more interested in the dogs we saw in the park than in the more exotic zoo animals—they were better suited to his age level and attention span. If you take a restless two-year-old to the *Nutcracker* or a three-year-old to a Disney movie before he is ready to sit still for long periods, neither of you will have much fun.

Toddlers are happier with simpler and more active excursions—a short ride on the bus, a trip to the bakery to select a cookie, a walk on a city street to look at buses and trucks, a stroll in the park or the woods to collect leaves, a chance to feed the ducks or float a boat on a pond. One-on-one activities that you share mean more than paid amusements.

If you are looking for entertainment, find a super playground or a children's museum with a special corner with play equipment just for tots.

Wherever you go, for best results, plan your outings after a nap so your grandchild will be fresh, and bring along a snack for refueling along the way.

Grandma and Grandpa's House

"It is wonderful for me to watch my mother so blissful with her grandchild. I feel more loved by her because she loves him so much."

As nice as it may be visiting your grandchild at his home, there's nothing like having that precious baby on your own turf. To see that this happens as often as possible, you want both children and parents to look forward to coming to see you. There are lots of things you can do to make these visits special for baby and relaxed for everyone.

The first is to remember that little children are noisy, restless, and inquisitive by nature. They aren't misbehaving if they say "no," and they will sometimes disobey. It is a normal part of growing up and asserting themselves. If parents feel you are critical of their children's behavior, they won't be anxious to visit.

That doesn't mean that you can't have rules and boundaries in your house, but recognize that until a child is at least two, he isn't going to fully understand and probably isn't always going to obey. And during those "terrible twos" it is a normal part of growing up to defy grown-ups, not a lack of parental discipline.

So don't make the parents feel you think they've failed if their children aren't letter-perfect. Stay relaxed and keep your sense of humor, enjoy the kids, and be glad you're a grandparent who doesn't have to deal with a toddler 24 hours a day.

BABY BAIT

If you want your grandchild to feel at home at your house, have a special box or basket in a closet where she knows she can go to find her toys (including an occasional surprise). Specific suggestions for toys for each age are in the reference section at the end of the book, but a few items like balls and blocks are favorites from infancy right through the toddler years and can be used in different ways as the child matures.

Don't forget that you probably have a ready supply of "toys" already. Big mixing bowls and plastic storage boxes are perfect during the phase when babies like putting things in and out of containers. Poker chips and a clean coffee can also make a great dumping and refilling toy. Nesting measuring cups and spoons, old pots and wooden spoons will keep baby happily occupied while you work in the kitchen. Cardboard shoe boxes with the tops taped on make great building blocks, or you can cut off the ends of a box bottom and create a tunnel. Large cartons can serve as a playhouse or a store counter for older toddlers.

My friend Fran entertained her two-year-old granddaughter for an hour with an old silk scarf, turning it into hats, dresses, and Superman capes for her dolls. Another friend has created a dress-up box filled with grown-up jackets, ties, and shoes and lots of beads for her grandson.

A surprise box is one grandparent's standby when children need distractions. A magnifying glass, a magnet, and bubble liquid are some of the things she recommends to fascinate toddlers. Small inexpensive plastic animals (especially dinosaurs and other creatures found at museum gift shops) are always favorites. Buy them in twos; toddlers like marching around pairs of little objects, one in each hand.

Jackson's favorite place in my house used to be a low shelf where he could help himself to his favorite books. He still likes to read, but once I bought some children's music tapes and taught him how to play them, the tape deck is now the first place he runs when he arrives. Watching my grandson dance around to the music is delicious. A child's tape recorder makes a great gift if you are a bit nervous about having him use your equipment.

Entertaining Little Ones

Have you forgotten what to do to entertain a toddler? Not to worry. One of the great charms about young children is that even ordinary things seem new and wonderful to them. Go to the store to shop for a meal, picking up a little treat along the way. At home, put on music and dance with your grandchild. Show him how a magnifying glass or a magnet works. Children love imitating grownups, so let them help you dust the furniture or dig in the garden; sort socks or empty the wastebaskets—they consider these chores as games. One much-loved grandpa lets his grandson lather and "shave" with him, using an old bladeless razor.

Little ones love using cookie cutters, whether on real cookie dough or play dough. Here's a recipe for making your own play dough at home:

Put ½ cup salt into 2 cups of water and boil until the salt dissolves. Stir in food coloring. Add 2 tablespoons salad oil, 2 cups sifted all-purpose flour, and 2 tablespoons of alum (available at the drugstore). Knead until you get an even consistency. Keep in an airtight container or a plastic bag, and it will last for about two months.

Time alone with your grandchildren is the best way to really get to know each other, so baby-sitting benefits both generations. However, you'll find that it is work as well as fun to take care of an infant, and that having a toddler for a full day or a weekend will leave you newly sympathetic to the energy required for parenting. When you are baby-sitting a toddler for a full day or longer, scout out a good playground where little ones can work off energy. Even if you don't approve of television, on rainy days a videotape may save the day, providing a quiet activity when children get tired and cranky. If you find that long caretaking sessions are more than you can handle, you should be honest with your children. Let them know that half a day or a few hours together is what you can handle. It doesn't mean that you don't love them or your grandchildren, only that you know your own limitations.

READY FOR COMPANY

If your grandchild visits often, you may well want to invest in some equipment so that bringing the baby isn't such a chore for parents. After all, the easier the trip, the more likely they are to come! The two most important items to own are a portable crib and a booster seat. You may be able to save by buying equipment at garage sales and consignment stores, but if you do, make sure anything you buy is sturdy, safe, and in good repair.

A group of four mothers in Salem, Oregon, each with young grandchildren who visit only once or twice each year, decided to pool their resources in a grandmothers' co-op. Each bought one of the more expensive items—crib, high chair, car seat, stroller—and stocked up on a few toys and books. When one of them has company, she has use of all the essentials. If you want to use their idea, they advise that you agree in advance on how to divide things if visits overlap, especially at the holidays.

The most popular portable crib is the Pack 'n Play made by Graco, also mentioned as a top gift for parents (see page 147). It is lightweight and folds compactly into its own bag to be stored in a corner of the closet when baby goes home.

If you prefer a more substantial wooden portable crib, features to look for are a flip-down side, which makes for less bending, and wheels so you can easily move it around the house. (Just be sure the side is never left down when baby is in the crib.) Adjustable legs are a plus; they take up less space when folded and you can lower the crib to floor level to use as a playpen. If you get a crib from a tag or garage sale, check that the slats are close enough together so that the baby can't get her head caught between them. The buying guide listed on pages 185–86 has more safety tips.

"Bouncy seats" are very useful before babies can sit up by themselves, though not essential for grandma's house, since their life span is only about six months. But once baby can sit up, booster seats for mealtime are indispensable, something you will use for a couple of years at a minimum.

Boosters are really cutoff high chairs that strap securely onto regular chairs. They have safety straps to keep tots securely seated and come with detachable feeding trays; the trays can be removed to allow toddlers to join the grown-ups at the table. The most practical models have plastic trays that can go into the dishwasher, a feature you'll appreciate more after you see the mess a toddler makes. Some have adjustable seat heights. Since they are much more compact than high chairs, boosters are easily unstrapped and stashed away in a closet when baby isn't around.

If you have the cash and the space, you can buy fancier seats, such as a high chair that converts into a play table when baby grows up a bit. If these aren't available in a local store, look for them and for other kinds of double-duty equipment in the catalogs on pages 179–80.

Since I see my grandchild once a week, I found it easiest for everybody to have a couple of bottles, nonbreakable baby dishes, and training cup and bib on hand. It was a minor investment that turned out to be a big convenience for my daughter, who doesn't have to remember to bring these things every week. And I had fun picking out the dishes, festooned with trains and boats that my grandson loves.

Some old-fashioned accessories are still very much in vogue for grandparents. There's nothing like a rocking chair for happy cuddling and lulling baby to sleep, and a cookie jar is quickly recognized by youngsters as the place to look for special treats.

BABY-SITTING BOO-BOOS

It's a grandparent's prerogative to be able to spoil the kids, but if you want to stay on the good side of parents don't overdo sweets and treats. Parents' wishes about what they want their child to eat need to be respected, and many parents today don't want their youngsters to have sugar or additives in their food. You may have to learn to substitute bananas or unsweetened apple sauce for chocolate chip cookies.

It's well to discuss in advance other rules that parents feel should be enforced. If they want an infant to sleep on his back, honor their wishes even though you always put your babies on their stomachs. If they are trying to wean their toddler from a bottle to a cup, don't sabotage them—even if you think he's too young to have his bottle taken away. The same goes for pacifiers, thumb-sucking, and security blankets—let her parents decide when it's time for her to stop.

PLAYING SAFE

Nothing puts parents on edge more than having to constantly be on guard that children don't damage grandma and grandpa's valuables or get into trouble crawling around. Everything is fair game for these eager little explorers, and babies tend to test things with their mouths as well as their hands. You don't have to go overboard every time baby comes to visit, but a one-time safety inspection and some simple precautions will allow everyone to be more relaxed when inquisitive crawlers and toddlers come to call.

The best way to inspect is to get down on your hands and knees and take a look at the temptations that a crawling baby will encounter. If you spy paper clips, screws, safety pins, coins, or other objects small enough to go into the mouth, get them out of the way in a hurry.

Sharp furniture corners can make for nasty bumps and bruises, but bumper cushions of soft foam will safeguard baby. Electrical outlets need to be filled with blank plugs, removing the temptation to poke at the open spaces, and lamp and appliance cords should be tacked down along baseboards. If hot water pipes or radiators are accessible, they need to be insulated or blocked by furniture.

Be sure that scatter rugs either have a nonskid backing or

are fastened with two-sided tape so that baby won't slide into trouble—and you won't trip while carrying him.

The cabinets under the kitchen sink can be lethal, as they are filled with ammonia, bleach, detergents, insecticides, and a dozen other hazardous products. Put whatever you can in a higher location. If an inquisitive toddler comes calling often, risky lower cabinets can be fitted with safety latches. Lid locks will keep little ones from dropping toys into the toilet bowl or playing in the water. You might want to make a small investment in a latch for the refrigerator, as well. Latches for doors or toilets are easy for you to open, but require more dexterity than a small child can manage.

These various safety devices are inexpensive and can be found in the baby aisles in some large supermarkets and drugstores or in the baby catalogs found on pages 179–80.

Check your closets as well as the cupboards. Shoe polish and plastic dry cleaner bags are just a few of the hazards that may be lurking on closet floors.

After a child can reach the windowsill, it's well to get into the habit of opening windows from the top, unless you have guardrails on the bottom half. Screens should always be in good repair, and the pull-cords on venetian blinds should be tied out of reach. You can buy cord wind-ups that keep the extra cord out of the way without interfering with normal use. Gates for your stairs will guard against nasty falls.

Once your grandchild can pull up to a standing position, low tabletops come in for inspection. This time you are safeguarding your valuables as well as the baby. You can either clear away breakables or try to teach your little explorer not to touch. I think it's easier to put fragile things away until the child is old enough to understand their value; otherwise, you can find yourself too busy saying "no" to have fun together.

To safeguard your books and CDs, pack them tightly into shelves so their contents are hard to remove, or move them to a higher spot.

Toddlers are curious about everything, and they often reach for things that can get them into trouble. When you are cooking with a little one around, use the back burners on the stove whenever you can. When you do need the front burners, always be sure that pot handles are turned away from the edge and out of reach. Needless to say, knives should be kept safe, on a magnetic bar placed high on the wall or in a wooden block that can be stored at the back of the counter.

If you take medicines, be extra careful to keep them where little fingers can't get at them. Don't rely on tamperproof tops to keep them safe. One mother who stored orange-flavored baby aspirin on a shelf in a high kitchen cabinet told me about her two-and-a-half-year-old daughter pulling a chair up to the kitchen counter, climbing up, uncapping the "childproof" bottle, and eating everything in the jar, sending the whole family off on a trip to the emergency room.

I just read a similar item in a parenting magazine, a warning by a grandmother whose 18-month-old granddaughter had climbed on top of a dresser to reach a shelf with her grandma's medicine and imitated grandma taking the tablets. Luckily grandma had a bottle of syrup of ipecac on hand to induce vomiting, so she was ready when the local poison control center advised her to use it.

Even with the best of care, accidents do happen on occasion, so if you sometimes take care of the baby, the purchase of a basic first-aid book is a reassuring addition to your library. If you haven't had to deal with bumps and bruises for a while, read through the book ahead of time so you'll know what to do and what to put on minor cuts and insect stings. Posting a simple first-aid chart is helpful, since it's so easy to forget what to do when you are trying to comfort a hurt, crying child. Some grandparents who care for their grandchildren say they enrolled in CPR classes for their own peace of mind. (Contact your local Red Cross for information on classes.)

Don't leave your young grandchild alone with your cat or dog; no matter how friendly and placid your pet may be, it isn't used to little ones who may poke an eye or a mouth out of curiosity. In fact, don't leave a child alone, period. Tots are notoriously creative about the mischief they find.

Having taken sensible steps to forestall serious trouble, however, you can then sit back and enjoy the adventures of your curious little explorer as she begins to get acquainted with the world around her. And if baby encounters a few inevitable minor bumps and spills along the way, try to remember that they probably hurt you more than they hurt her.

Safety First

As part of your safety check, be ready for emergencies by seeing that the medicine cabinet is stocked with the following:

- Band-Aids
- antiseptic and other first-aid supplies for cuts
- baby acetominophen
- a baby thermometer
- syrup of ipecac

When you are in charge, be sure that easy-to-see emergency numbers are beside the telephone. Include the following:

- baby's doctor
- emergency medical and ambulance services
- the fire department
- a poison-control center

How to Parent New Parents

"We never criticize," says the grandmother. "We bite our tongues and keep quiet."

"They don't exactly criticize," says the mother. "They make comments—loaded comments."

For most families, a new generation is a bond that draws everyone closer. It gives new parents more understanding of what their own parents went through and grandparents a new view of their children as responsible adults. As one Massachusetts mother said with a laugh, "Now we always have something to talk about."

Grandparents feel enormous pride seeing their children measure up as parents. "My daughter was older, had married late, and she had a demanding job and a busy way of life before deciding to have children. I wasn't sure how she would handle it," one Pennsylvania grandmother admits. "But she's a wonderful, loving mother, and I really admire the way she is able to manage her complicated life."

"I was truly moved seeing how involved my son is in the

care of his daughter," a New Hampshire grandmother relates. "I would never have predicted it."

Most young families say that grandparents who live nearby are a godsend, providing practical help and moral support when parents really need it. And almost every parent said they had expected and hoped the grandparents would be actively involved with their children, and were thrilled when this occurred. "I looked at my mother rocking the baby and I thought, 'This is what she must have been like with me,' " said one new mother. "It made me love her more."

Most of those interviewed definitely appreciated having parents on hand after the birth of the baby, though a few did prefer having the first week or two for themselves and then having a parent spend time with them.

The arrival of a baby in the family isn't all smooth sailing, however. New parents are nervous. They want to do everything right, but they are novices and they often seem most defensive when they are most unsure. What they crave most is support, assurance that they are doing well. They want their own parents to be pleased and proud of their performance as parents. Any hint of disapproval rankles.

Parents who think they have accepted the fact that their adult children have different values and lifestyles often discover it is harder to approve once their children become parents. "The hardest part of being a grandparent is when you don't agree with the way the parents are raising the kids," says one grandmother.

Her son comments, "I'm 35 years old, and I thought my

parents had accepted my lifestyle, which is quite different from theirs. But since the baby, I feel like they are saying, 'O.K., now it's time to grow up and be like me.' "

Part of the problem is that the world has changed so much. Most grandparents were brought up in a time when parents were strict and children were expected to be "good." Many raised their infants on inflexible schedules of three- and four-hour feedings, and they watch their grandchildren being fed on demand, regardless of the inconvenience to the parents. "That baby is never allowed to cry," one grandmother comments. "Maybe it's better than the way we did things and he will be more secure, as my children say, but I can't help but think he's going to be spoiled."

Grandparents also worry about the effects of day care. "The biggest problem I had with my parents was their trying to convince me to stay home with my baby because it is such an important time of his life," one working mother in New York comments. "They just don't seem to understand that we need my income to pay the mortgage. I feel guilty enough without them adding to it."

Grandparents are also concerned that youngsters today are pushed too fast. "The biggest change I see is the fast pace kids keep these days," says one grandfather. "From day care centers to churches to gyms to television, they are pushed to learn almost from the time they can talk."

What's New?

Here's what grandparents say are the biggest changes they see since their own parenting days, clues to what may lie ahead for you:

• "Fathers are so much more involved. I was amazed to see my son changing diapers, feeding the baby, even taking time off from work to go to the pediatrician along with the mother when the baby has his monthly checkup. I know two families where the father stays home with the baby because the mother has the better-paying job."

• "Parents are more relaxed about timetables, don't rush taking away the bottle or toilet training as we did. But they also don't enforce as many rules, so kids are not as well behaved."

• "I was a stay-at-home mother who loved getting vacations away from the kids. My daughter is a working mom, and she and her husband would never think of going away without her daughter. They rarely even use babysitters—they take her everywhere."

• "The intrusion of popular culture is producing a generation of children who seem to know a lot but don't understand what they see. I think they are exposed to too much too soon."

• "Working mothers are the biggest change. In my day, it was the parents who sacrificed for the children; now it seems to me that children who spend their days in day care are doing the sacrificing."

• "Safety is an issue we never faced. My daughter and her friends on a nice suburban block will never leave their toddlers in the backyard alone. That would never have occurred to me."

• "Much of the job is easier today—no more boiling bottles, sterilizing formula, or folding diapers. At the same time, families are more stressed because both parents are working. They have guilt we didn't feel."

Parents have always taken their responsibilities seriously, but because they tend to be older now, they seem more conscientious and almost too concerned to some members of the older generation. Several grandparents made the same comment, "They seem to read so much and worry so much—we just did it."

Parents admit that they bristle when grandparents tell them to lighten up, or make comments like "We used playpens and it didn't hurt anyone," or "We insisted on two naps a day and the kids just had to stay in that bed."

What is happening here is an age-old conflict when children grow up and parents no longer have control, a shift heightened by the start of a new generation. Well-meaning grandparents may be genuinely concerned or may fear their children are making mistakes, but it is difficult to express their concerns. They have to learn to cope with feelings of powerlessness.

They have to understand that the new parents are also in a transitional state. Parenthood, the shift from being a child to caring for a child, is the final step to full adulthood and it is scary. Still not confident as parents, they are torn between wanting to be independent yet not wanting to totally lose their comfortable dependent roles. One minute they may be calling for advice, the next resenting your interference. Grandparents must strike a delicate balance between being available for advice and not feeling resentful when that advice is not taken.

Even though they think they are refraining from criticizing, grandparents often manage to convey their feelings in a way that children resent even more than open discussion. "My parents think they don't give advice," says one mother. "But they make loaded comments. 'Jenny looks tired; I wonder if she is spending too many hours in day care,' or 'Is there any toy that this child does not have?' Things like that come across to me as criticism. I get defensive. I feel like a child all over again."

Many young parents say flatly that parents should follow the old adage, "If you can't say something good, don't say anything." But parents who have real concerns find it hard to constantly bite their tongues. Helen Block Fields, an educator and intergenerational consultant who led a grandparent support group in Illinois for eight years, found many grandparents suffering from what she describes as "chronic sore tongues and stiff necks" from never voicing their concerns to their adult children, always turning the other cheek. They hesitated to be open and honest because they feared their children would take offense and punish them by distancing their grandchildren.

When you are seriously concerned about an issue that you

feel is harmful to your grandchild, you should discuss it, Fields believes. "But don't put anyone on the defensive," she advises. "Use 'I' not 'you.' If something is bothering you, say, 'I'm worried about . . .' or 'I don't understand . . . Will you explain to me?'

"Always speak in a caring, noncritical way," she continues. "If the issue is very sensitive, perhaps write down your words ahead of time and rehearse to yourself so you keep excess emotion out of your statements. Once you've said your piece, then drop it. Don't keep bringing it up. Whether to follow your advice is their decision."

Parents agree that they wish grandparents who don't approve of some of their practices would ask questions in a tactful way, aiming to better understand the reasons why they are doing certain things. "I only wish my mother would ask me to explain why I want to breast-feed rather than just saying, 'I don't know why you are going through all that work,' " is one typical young mother's comment. "Ideas change, sometimes for the better. Find out what the current thinking is."

Many parents say they would happily offer things to read so grandparents would better understand their parenting strategies—if the grandparents would only ask.

One young mother decided to invite the child's grandmother along to monthly checkups with the pediatrician. "When I tell her things, she tends to argue that old ways are the best. When she hears it from the doctor, she accepts it," says the mother.

Still, one of the lessons grandparents must learn is to sit back and be silent most of the time, because they have to accept that they are not in charge. "Save your advice for important things, things you feel could really harm the child," advises Helen Block Fields. "Don't fight small battles. Win the war."

"I've had to recognize that somebody else has ultimate responsibility, and learn to take my lead from them," one grandmother acknowledges. "I try not to undercut their discipline. One small example: their rule is that a two-year-old must finish his milk before he leaves the table. I think he's too young to understand what they are trying to do, but I know better than to try to change the rules or interfere. I just love my grandson and enjoy him, and let his parents be in charge of discipline. In fact, I find that not having to discipline is one of the great joys of grandparenting!"

Grandparents who take care of their grandchildren regularly have even more opportunities for disagreement. "I really appreciate the fact that my mother-in-law takes the baby so often, but we are trying to move him from a bottle to a cup and she insists on giving him a bottle because *she* thinks he is too young," is one mother's complaint.

To avoid conflicts, grandparents need to ask the parents to spell out what is not negotiable when it comes to matters such as eating, naps, bedtime, and discipline, and to honor their feelings. Knowing that the important rules are being followed, it is up to the parents then to relax and realize that grandparents are supposed to be softies, that it is O.K. if they spoil the children a bit or do things in their own way. Parents sometimes fear that children will be spoiled or confused by the differences in style and behavior of grandparents, but even toddlers can easily distinguish between the two households, and you can reassure them that what you do will not undermine their discipline. You might remind them that grandparents are important in children's lives precisely because they are different from parents—because they give a different perspective along with the deep love that adds to a child's sense of security.

Baby-sitting can become an issue if grandparents feel they are being imposed on. Grandmothers, who are usually the baby-sitters, agree that you can't allow yourself to be taken for granted. Parents need to have backup sitters and not assume you will always be available.

"If you feel you are being taken advantage of, you will resent the time with your grandchild," advises a veteran grandma. "If you are honest when you want time for yourself, then your children, in turn, can be open about telling you if you are visiting too often, and everyone feels more comfortable. The best arrangement if you live close by seems to be having a regular date that is convenient for you. Then parents can depend on you and make their own plans accordingly."

Providing baby-sitting that allows the new parents time alone together is one way grandparents can help with the reworking of family relationships that comes with the arrival of a new baby. "When a couple marries, they set up visiting patterns and boundaries that are necessary to separate from their parents and allow them to forge their own household," according to Nancy Wasserman Cocola, a psychotherapist and author of *Six in the Bed*. "With best intentions and out of excitement and love for the infant, grandparents may view the birth of a child as license to overstep these boundaries. They want more time with the new family, and may even begin to pop in unexpectedly."

These unannounced visits come at the same time that new parents are renegotiating their own marital relationship, she reminds. Grandparents have to recognize that the first priority for parents must be to establish their new family. "The more you let go as a parent, the more respectful you are of the new family's privacy, the more likely they are to be generous to you," Cocola counsels.

The new family will appreciate your efforts to be friendly with the other set of grandparents. When you can, avoid making the children choose between you for visits. Most families work out an alternating schedule for holidays, but where it is geographically possible, it can be better for the young family to suggest that all of you get together occasionally. Otherwise, as one mother says, "To keep both families happy, it means that we are always traveling for the major holidays. It is wearing and expensive and makes it stressful all around."

Competition between sets of grandparents for favor with the baby is a common problem reported by parents. "Each grandmother asks what the other has sent, and then tries to outdo it," reports one mother. "If my father hears that the other grandfather took the kids to the zoo, you can be sure that's where he will take them the next time they visit," says another.

Even grandparents who like the other family admit to feeling a touch of rivalry. "It does bother me that my granddaughter seems to favor her other grandmother," an Illinois woman says. "I wonder if she's secretly sneaking her candy."

A little bit of rivalry is natural, but some parents find that it gets out of hand. "My husband's parents acted like they wanted to be the only grandparents," says an Ohio mother.

"They want him all the time. My father-in-law turned into an absolute monster because we named the baby after him. He has calmed down now, but only after we had many talks."

"Come Christmas, our families overwhelm us with presents for the baby, each wanting to be more generous than the other," says another parent. "Our daughter has more clothes than she could wear in two lifetimes. It would be great if, instead of competing, they would sometimes go in together for a big present like an outdoor swing set."

Grandparents are only human, and we make mistakes, just as our children will with their own families. But happily, most parents accept us as we are and are simply happy that we care. So do your best to be tactful, but most of all heed the advice of one young mother: "Be there. Jump in. Most families welcome the involvement and are touched by it. They would rather have some unwanted advice than have you be hands-off."

Advice from New Parents

• "Keep your mouth shut the first couple of times you go to see the baby except to say how beautiful she is. This is not the time to criticize what the house looks like, or how tired your child is. Don't give advice—ask what you can do to help. But be ready to be gracious if your child turns you down. The parents may want these first weeks to themselves."

• "As your kids adjust to parenthood, let them bask in their newfound techniques for dealing with baby. Sure you realize the baby is tired, wet, etc., but soon the parents will figure it out, as well."

• "Never drop in without calling, and ask for the same respect from your children. Stress that they don't have to entertain you when you visit. Instead, try to be helpful. Ask if you can take the baby for a walk, giving mom a break. Offer to baby-sit so parents can have dinner out."

• "Instead of giving presents, give of yourself. Bring over a home-cooked meal or offer to do the laundry. If the baby can be fed with a bottle, one of the best things you can do for parents who haven't had a full night's sleep in weeks is to offer to keep the baby overnight on a Saturday so they can sleep in on Sunday morning."

• "When they are having problems with the baby at home, don't keep telling them how well she ate or slept for you."

• "Be ready with a sympathetic ear, but don't give advice unless it is asked for. Instead of offering solutions, reassure—have faith they will figure it out."

• "Don't encourage unwanted hand-me-downs from relatives."

• "Learn from your children, don't always be trying to teach them."

• "Trust your children's judgment. Times have changed and we parents are aware of things grandparents were not aware of years ago. It doesn't mean that we are better parents, but we are trying hard. Understand that your grandchildren probably won't be raised exactly like your kids were. Offer advice on anything you feel very strongly, but don't force the point if it is not well received. Remember that ultimately your child is in charge, not you. Enjoy your grandchild and just give us some space and let us enjoy our turn at parenting."

The Long-Distance Grandparent

"I'm determined that distance isn't going to keep me from being close to my grandchild."

The days when Grandma and Grandpa lived down the block are long gone for many families. In our mobile society, young adults tend to follow career opportunities, so long-distance grandparenting is a fact of life for many families. But just because your children live far away doesn't mean you can't be a close part of your grandchild's life. It takes effort, but those who've done it have lots of tips to share on how to stay in touch. It's possible to form an early connection even with the very young, and find ways to visit so that they can bond with your voice and face.

Even during the first year, before you can really communicate, you can find ways to make yourself familiar to your grandchild. "Infants see best at first in black and white, so I started with a big black-and-white photo that my daughter placed near the changing table," one grandmother advises.

Many grandparents tape lullabies and nursery rhymes to be played for the baby. "Don't worry about being out of tune," advises one doting grandpa. "The baby won't mind."

A Michigan grandmother uses her tapes to pass on family traditions. "I get so much pleasure repeating the songs that my father had sung to me, and that I had sung to my daughter. As my grandchild got older, a kiddy tape recorder was one of the best presents I ever gave her. Now she not only listens, but sends her own tapes back to me."

Another grandmother suggests reading a book into the tape, choosing a book the baby already has or sometimes sending a new book along with the tape. She makes it more fun by ringing a little bell at the end of each page and instructing, "Turn the page."

Grandma can also tell her own stories, and later ask questions that the children can answer on a return tape. As the children get older, they will very much look forward to these tape exchanges.

When baby is old enough to listen to the telephone, you can repeat some of the songs and rhymes, and you'll soon be recognized when you call. "My daughter tells me my seven-month-old grandson smiles when he hears me sing 'Frere Jacques,' and I feel I've made a connection even though he lives in Seattle and I'm in Tampa," one pleased grandmother says.

Selma Wasserman, in her book, *The Long Distance Grandmother*, tells how she connected with her grandson via telephone, beginning when he was six months old. She called regularly and had his mother hold the phone to the baby's ear while she asked, "Where is your nose? Where are your pretty little eyes? Where are your sweet little toes?"—the same questions he was hearing often from his mom and dad. By the time the baby was a year old, the calls were a regular fixture in his routine, and he responded to her by echoing the words "nose," "eyes," or "toes." And when she said, "I'm going to kiss those little toes . . . kiss, kiss, kiss," she heard "the most delicious, delightful, delectable giggle of pleasure that will sing in your ears and warm your heart."

As grandchildren grow old enough to have a conversation, you can have a regular telephone date that they will wait for each week. This should be their own personal call, not an add-on to a conversation with Mommy and Daddy. Make sure that the time of the call is one that is convenient for parents, and be prepared to do most of the talking, since tykes with limited vocabularies like listening better than talking. They do love hearing your voice and hearing "I love you" even from afar. When Jackson says, "Hi, Grandma," to me into the phone, the sound is sweeter than music!

By age three when children are more verbal, you can have a real conversation, though you're still going to have to keep things going by asking the right questions. Keep up with their doings through their parents so that you have something to talk about. I have to smile when one of my executive friends repeats with glee the funny things her grandson says to her on the phone. Along with the anecdotes, she gets a wonderful bonus—a little voice saying, "I miss you, Grandma."

When you say, "I love you," and hear "I love you, too, Grandma," without coaching from parents, it is a gift beyond compare. "The first time I heard it," says one grandmother, "I cried."

Don't take it personally if your toddler grandchild occasionally doesn't want to talk on the phone. Remember that toddlers often say no just because they need to assert themselves. I overheard a woman on the bus complaining because her daughter didn't insist that her granddaughter had to come to the telephone. "I think it's shameful. She needs to discipline that child," said Grandma. I could only smile and think that Grandma had forgotten what it was like to live through the "terrible twos." Be assured that before long your phone calls will be wonderfully welcome.

A video camera is the best selfish gift a distant grandparent can give to new parents. It will allow you to share the moments you miss—the baby crawling or taking first steps. And a camera of your own can be just as valuable. It is one of the best ways to let your grandchild get to know you from afar. One creative grandmother dresses up in costumes and has herself taped reading children's stories. Another sends a videotape of herself baking cookies—and has it arrive about the same time that the cookies do.

By the time toddlers turn two and have become more aware, you can do more with videotape. Walk her around your house—show her where she will sleep when she comes to visit, where you will work in the garden together, where you will fix her dinner. If you have pets, be sure to introduce your cat or dog.

When you are together, have someone tape you doing things with your grandchild so she can watch the video later and remember you. If she comes to your house, record some of the fun things you do so she can replay them at home.

If your children have a fax machine at home and you own or have access to one, these are wonderful high-tech communicators for distant grandparents. Even at age one, little ones think it's magical watching the message come through. Send a drawing or a picture or big letters spelling her name—she'll love it.

You don't have to be into high tech to be someone special to your grandchildren, however. A grandmother in North Carolina makes cloth books and sends them to her baby granddaughter in Virginia. "Now that she is older, she calls them her 'quiet books,'" Grandma reports with pleasure. "One of her favorites was a story about a zebra because I sent a homemade zebra along with the book." Fabrics imprinted with book pages are available in fabric stores, she reports; the seamstress simply puts interfacing between each page.

Another grandmother suggests stitching together rectangles of solid color cloth and sending them with a box of markers for little ones to make their own books by drawing scribbles and pictures on each page.

One grandmother sends a monthly box to her grandchildren who live in another country with a scrapbook of photos and souvenirs of what Grandma and Grandpa have been doing that month. She includes coupons good for visits to the circus or the zoo on their annual visit. She narrates the pages with a tape. The parents, in turn, have the children make up a scrapbook to send back.

By the time children are three, they can begin to appreciate another very special book from a grandparent—a little family album of their own, filled with photos (or copies or photocopies of photos you don't want to give away). You can trace the child from baby to big boy, or do pictures of Daddy or Mommy and uncles and aunts as babies and toddlers. Do simple captions that parents can read to the child—and that he can later read to himself.

Some other grandparent suggestions for keeping in touch:

• From about 18 months, send postcards regularly. Little ones adore getting mail and will soon learn to watch for the postman. You don't have to be on a trip. Send a picture of a baby or a flower, write a short message—"Isn't he cute?" or "Isn't this pretty?" and sign it, "I love you and I miss you, Grandpa." Or send a picture of an animal and say, "Next time you come to see me, we'll go to visit this guy at the zoo." One grandmother writes a postcard every day in order to remain a constant presence in her grandchild's life.

• Send picture books about children and grandparents with a picture of yourself tucked in—or even better, a picture of the two of you.

• Send a box of old dresses, discarded necklaces, suits and ties as dress-ups, so toddlers can play being Grandma or Grandpa.

• Send a packet of seeds to be planted and ask for pictures to be sent when they come up. Some families plant twin gardens, one in the child's backyard, the other at the grandparents' home. Then they compare progress by mailing photos or drawings to each other.

• Participate in birthdays and holidays even when you can't be there in person. Send Easter egg coloring, a Halloween mask, or ornaments for the Christmas tree. Provide the favors or the hats for your grandchild's party.

• As children get older, share a story. Grandparents can write the first lines and send them for the child to continue and send back. Some families have stories that keep going back and forth for weeks.

• Pay attention to children of a similar age in your family or neighborhood so you'll have some idea of the stages your grandchild is going through. Even though each child is different, it will help you gauge what to buy and how to play with your grandchild when you see him.

• Create a family tree with pictures that include everyone in the family and send it to your grandchild to help make her familiar with you as well as with aunts and uncles who may live far away.

COMING TO VISIT

Of course, you'll want to visit as often as you can—but eager though you may be to see the baby, both generations strongly suggest that you limit your stay. Even the most welcome company puts a strain on the family. Better to go home while everyone wishes you were staying longer! If you live within reasonable commuting distance, plan regular weekends rather than extended visits. If the distance is far and airfares are expensive, a week seems to be a safe choice.

If you are thinking of a longer trip, consider the situation honestly. How relaxed and comfortable are you and your children when you are together? Remember that longer visits present many more opportunities for each generation to get on the other's nerves. If there is an extra bedroom and bath, you will be less of a disturbance to the household than if you are sleeping on the living room couch or sharing a room with your grandchild. Households with young children start the day early, probably earlier than you are used to rising. Some grandparents who can afford it stay in a nearby motel or hotel to give both generations a break and some privacy.

Lots of grandparents tend to plan visits around holidays like Christmas or Easter, but if you can only come once or twice a year, many advise not always choosing these busy periods. They point out that you get a better picture of life when nothing special is happening, as well as more quiet time to visit and more one-on-one time with grandchildren.

Don't be hurt or disappointed if your grandchild doesn't rush to you at once. You are not a constant presence in her life and it may take time for a little one to warm up, so be prepared and let her make the first approaches rather than overwhelming her.

You're probably going to bring presents, but you don't have to spend a fortune to make your grandchild happy to see you.

"Instead of one big thing, I bring small things so there's a surprise every day," one grandma reports. Activities you can do together will help you forge bonds; bubble liquid or a jack-in-the-box are usually hits with tots; play dough and sticker books are good icebreakers with two- and three-year-olds.

You may be happy to do some baby-sitting to give the parents a break and have your grandchildren all to yourself, but if you are nervous about this because you don't know the child well, don't hesitate to say so. Nor need you let yourself be overloaded, or given a pile of chores you don't want to do. Your kids may think having you around is a great chance to be taken care of once again. If they have saved the mending or the gardening or a list of home repairs for you and you like being needed, great. But if you'd rather not, there's nothing wrong with saying, "I'm really sorry, but I'm just not feeling up to it right now." Don't become like the grandfather who puts off visits because each time he returns home exhausted from a round of house repairs.

Your visits will be far more welcome if you don't behave like a guest who needs to be entertained. "I hate it when my mother says to me, 'What are we going to do today?' " says a weary daughter. "I wish she'd just relax around the house, maybe take the baby for a walk to give me a break. I'm tired and the last thing I want to do is entertain company."

The cardinal sin visiting grandparents commit, their adult children agree, is trying to take over. Here are some typical complaints:

• "I can't stand it when my mother comes because she's compulsively neat and we're not. She just can't stand a dirty dish in the sink or toys on the floor, so she's constantly cleaning or picking up. She's forgotten what it's like to live with a toddler. She drives me crazy."

• "My mother takes over *my* kitchen," grouses another daughter. "She tells me how to cook, rearranges the cabinets, and if I say something, she's hurt and says she's only trying to be helpful."

• "My father is Mr. Fix-it, and as soon as he comes in the door, he starts looking for projects. This is fine, up to a point, but my husband has to rush around providing tools and supplies, and he doesn't like this. He also sometimes feels like this is a silent criticism of his own abilities. So he's never very happy to hear my folks are coming."

• "I dread my parents coming because I can sense they don't approve of the way we're raising the children. They think we are far too permissive. One example: We had to eat everything on our plates; I don't think it's an issue to fight over. Even when they don't say anything, I can see the looks they give each other."

How to avoid these stresses? "It's human nature to think some of your ways are better than your kids' lifestyle," advises one wise grandmother, "but you have to realize that you are dealing with adults. Try to forget that these are your children and pretend that you are visiting other adult friends. Abide by their household routines, and be sensitive to times when you are overstepping your role as a guest. You'd never go around picking up after your friends or criticize what they have for dinner. And you'd certainly never tell them how to raise their children!"

Grandparents and Computers

Once a child is able to read, there is no more instant, economical way to stay in touch than via E-mail—and no surer way to have your grandchild think you are hip! My nephew, who has a scanner, recently sent me an E-mail photo of his family that I could run off on my printer, a wonderful way to keep in touch.

Grandparents who don't come into the computer age are going to seem antediluvian, for by the time your grandchild is in kindergarten, he or she will almost surely be learning and playing games on the computer. The time to gain some basic skills is now, so that you'll be able to keep up. The cost of a basic computer has come way down, and lots of libraries and community colleges offer beginning courses to get you started.

Another good reason to have a computer: you can share experiences and problems with other grandparents on the Internet, as well as pick up do's and don'ts from parents who are talking about the grandparents in their families. Many people find it a great place to vent when their families are driving them crazy, and their complaints are instructive. Two great sources are *Parent Soup* and *Parents Place*, each with a long list of bulletin boards, including places especially for grandparents. See the full addresses on pages 186–87.

The Overextended Family

"My granddaughter was only two when my son told me he and his wife were separating. I felt as though the world had come to an end."

Of all the changes that complicate family relations, divorce can be the trickiest. Statistics tell us that 50 percent of marriages don't make it, and both the older and younger generations help make up these figures, presenting a new set of family logistics for everyone.

Today it isn't unusual for a newborn child to have divorced grandparents. Only too often, warring ex-spouses meet at the hospital to welcome their grandchild, a bittersweet moment that can quickly turn into tense resentment when new spouses are also on hand. The competition for love, the question of who gets holiday visits is doubly complicated for the parents, and the number of visits paid to the baby can become overwhelming to the household.

There are no easy answers to such complex relations. The best that can be hoped for is to form what Dr. Harold H.

Bloomfield calls a "parenting coalition" in his book, *Making Peace in Your Stepfamily*. One person must be big enough to take the lead, inviting the ex-spouse and new mate to lunch or dinner to acknowledge openly the mixed feelings, and the need to accept each other for the sake of the new baby and its parents. You can even go one step further. If there are uncles and aunts on all sides and the future great-grandparents are alive, you can get all the adults together, acknowledging that, for better or for worse, everyone is now "family" and the baby deserves love and attention from all.

Awkward though it may be, with sincere effort resentments can be put aside. I know a grandmother and grandfather who barely speak, yet both were present (and pleasant) with their daughter to watch their grandson being born.

"Both my husband and I have remarried, and we have all been able to talk to each other when there has been a problem and handled it with as much respect for the other as possible under the circumstances," another grandmother told me. "The key is putting priorities in their place and not letting personal feelings about the other get in the way, so the grandchildren can be happy to be with all of us. We've managed to keep free of visible tensions that are difficult for little ones to understand."

One grandmother credits her children with saving the situation. "They probably were a lot wiser than myself about all this—they told me they were not going to tell me things about their dad and for me not to ask—and they were not going to tell him things about me. That has eliminated a lot of jealousy and bickering back and forth."

A young mother told me, "I'm forever grateful to my mother for making peace with my father and his wife before the baby was born. They certainly don't love each other, but they do cooperate and tolerate each other for some holidays and for birthday parties so we don't have to make a choice. My father actually took a picture of everyone in the extended family at my son's first birthday, and I must say, it is in a frame in the most prominent place in my living room. I think this is the best gift they could have given the baby."

Because babies are so lovable, relating to new stepgrand-children does not seem to be a problem unless the step-grandparent has not been accepted by the parents, or the stepgrandparent tries to compete for love with the real grand-parents.

It is a little more complicated when you remarry and become an instant grandma or grandpa to an older child. You'll have to recognize that you may not be welcomed imme-diately with open arms, but over time, if you can establish a friendship with your stepgrandchildren, everyone will benefit. Common sense will tell you that you cannot and should not try to replace the real grandparent, but you can still be a uniquely special person in the child's life, with both genera-tions reaping warm rewards as a result. No child can have too many people who love him.

"My dad's new wife has actually made me closer to him," one mother says. "On his own, he wasn't really comfortable with his granddaughter, but his wife is great with children, and he's warmed up as a result. Even if he's only showing off for her, it makes me happy. Now we can look forward to his visits."

And a grandfather says, "To my surprise, I discovered when my grandson was born that I actually like my ex-wife's husband. It makes getting together a lot easier. At least I can talk to *him*."

Equally difficult and far sadder is the situation when young children are caught up in a divorce. Often grandparents say they are the last to know, since adult children find it hardest of all to admit the failure of their marriage to their parents. This is not the time to pass judgment on your child or the spouse. Your focus should be on the grandchild. Regardless of the circumstances, a grandparent's love does not end with a divorce, and the constancy of grandparents' presence can help immeasurably to ease the strains for children. Grandparents can provide a peaceful haven, a sense of normalcy, and extra hugs and attention at a crucial time. When children are old enough to understand, grandparents can help to explain that they haven't done anything wrong to cause the divorce, a common fear with youngsters. Many grandparents step in to offer much-needed child care and financial aid during a difficult transition period. Sometimes they even find themselves, unexpectedly, providing a home for child and grandchild.

Says one grandmother, "My divorced daughter and her three-year-old son have lived with us since he was five months old. He is a great child and we have benefited greatly having them with us. When people tell us what an admirable thing we have done for our daughter, I tell them it isn't admirable—it's what families are supposed to do. We do have to work hard to remember that this boy has a father and a mother, and not to overstep our place. But I love that little boy so—secretly I dread the day when they leave us!"

Grandparents can help out in many ways, but they cannot take sides in a divorce if they hope to be able to maintain a close relationship with the grandchildren. Anything negative you say about a parent hurts the child; children need to love both their parents.

When grandparents do openly side with one parent, there are damaging results, especially when the grandparents blame their own child for the divorce. "My mother-in-law has not even seen my baby in over six months though she lives in the same town," one mother reports. "She thought her son was wrong to leave his family and she has cut her ties with him. She ignores us, but she goes out of her way to visit his ex-wife and be generous with his daughter from the first marriage. It isn't just her son who feels badly about this. Our baby doesn't know the difference yet, but I have an eight-year-old from a previous marriage and she has had her feelings hurt over and over when my husband's daughter comes to visit every other weekend and brags about all the things she has gotten from her grandmother. It will be even worse when our baby is old enough to understand that his grandmother doesn't want to see him."

Since mothers usually have custody of the children in a divorce, it is often the paternal grandparents who stand to suffer the greatest loss. The first thing to be done is to approach the daughter-in-law to express your love for the child, and your hope to remain part of his life. "Keep the conversation geared to the needs of the child," says Helen Block Fields, a specialist in intergenerational issues. "Don't let either parent turn you into a go-between for anger between them."

Grandparents who have been through a family divorce warn you can't just assume that you will be free to see your grandchild as time goes on, especially if remarriage occurs. It is vital to see that you are included in the legal custody agreement, with visitation rights spelled out. If your child's lawyer cannot attain this for you because of bitterness with the divorcing spouse, you may have to hire your own attorney. Almost every state now has recognized the importance of the grandparental relationship and has laws that guarantee grandparents' visitation rights.

Because of divorce, desertion, and many other factors that may affect the parents, it is estimated that some four million children in the United States currently live in a household headed by a grandparent. For over 1.5 million of these children, no parent is present and the grandparents have taken on the responsibility for the grandchildren. Often they are acting without legal sanction but they are caring for their grandchildren because the parents have illnesses, mental problems, or addictions preventing them from coping with their children.

The full-time challenge of raising grandchildren is difficult for many reasons, and a number of communities now have formed support groups for these grandparents. The AARP Grandparent Information Center in Washington, D.C., was formed in 1993 to serve as a national resource center. In its very first year of operation, it reported over 4,700 requests for information and referrals to local support programs. The Center can be reached at (202) 434-2296.

The world is changing so dramatically that many grandparents find themselves facing issues that were rare or unheard of only a few decades ago. One woman wrote me that she would soon be grandmother to a baby that will be raised by her daughter and her female partner. The partner was pregnant through a donor, via a sperm bank in California. Her daughter, a songwriter, has written a song called "Love on a Credit Card," all about how the baby will be grown by the time the Visa bill for the sperm is paid. Says the future grandmother, "I know this baby will receive a lot of love and that she will be very special in my life. I would like to share this story with others."

A grandmother in the Midwest shared her feelings of awkwardness because her son and his girlfriend decided not to marry after the birth of their son. "We are all trying to work together so the baby has the love of all of us and grows up to feel loved and secure," she says.

Though she is close to both parents and both often ask for advice, she notes, "It is a sticky situation when the parents are not married. I am always afraid that I might lose my grandson, so we are always loving, neutral, and caring to everyone concerned. We do not take sides and do not preach, and the baby's mother knows we love her, too. I really wish his parents would get married. I want him to have the best possible life."

Another matter that divides some families is intermarriage between race or religions, a far more frequent occurrence than in the past. Grandparents may feel a deep sense of loss knowing that a grandchild will be raised with unfamiliar cultural values, in a different religion or with no religion at all, but to make an issue of this is to risk alienating the parents.

Even within the same religion, the customs of a christening

or bris may be more important to grandparents than to the parents. You can discuss your feelings frankly, but the final decision is with the parents, and you have little choice other than to swallow your disappointment and accept their decision gracefully. This is another instance where grandparents must recognize that they are no longer in control.

Intermarriage may turn out to be a good experience if you allow yourself to be open, to broaden your horizons, and to share some of the customs of the new family members.

You may also be able to suggest some new customs that are unique to your family and show respect for everyone. Understanding that ceremony is important to their parents, some young families have created their own lovely rituals such as naming ceremonies as substitutes for the usual religious ones. These ceremonies are sometimes held in Ethical Culture, Unitarian, or Quaker churches, which welcome all religions, or sometimes take place at home. One beautiful ceremony that I read about began with parents welcoming the guests, who were immediate family and closest friends. Then the mother told the story of the child's birth and the father told the origin of her name. Friends read poems about the love that children awaken. Members of the immediate family then bestowed small symbolic gifts for the baby. Last, everyone formed a circle, music was played, and the baby was passed slowly from person to person for a special wish, a kiss, and sometimes a blessing. Afterwards lunch was served. "Even my husband's Catholic parents were moved by the ceremony," the mother said.

Complicated family relationships raise emotional and

sometimes explosive issues that are frequently difficult to deal with alone. Family counseling can be helpful, and you may find a community organization that will help you organize a support group for grandparents similar to those that exist for stepparents.

But in the end it remains up to individuals to muster the love, goodwill, and acceptance that can allow a family to survive and thrive, no matter how untraditional its form may be. The love and joy that accompanies the birth of a baby can help to bring this about.

The Family Tree

Families may be more complicated, but however overextended, they are still families. You can show your goodwill by collecting photos to create a "family tree" for baby that includes everyone, including steprelations. The process of creating the tree may help you to accept the hard fact that people you don't know will be family to your grandchild.

The Reluctant Grandparent

"I didn't feel old enough to be a grandmother, and I didn't want the role."

Nothing makes a new parent sadder than to realize that the grandparents aren't really interested in their baby. While the majority of grandparents are thrilled with their new roles and want to be closely involved with their grandchildren, not everyone feels the same instant overwhelming love for an infant. There are many reasons. Here's what some grandparents said:

- "I was only 41 when my daughter became pregnant. I had hardly finished raising my own children, and I wasn't ready for any more."

- "I was disappointed in myself. I'd expected to feel the same thrill that all my friends had experienced, but I just didn't. It made me search my feelings and admit that I really was not a person who particularly liked mothering small children. I'm afraid it's just the way I am."

• "Having had an unhappy relationship with my daughter-in-law, who clearly doesn't like me, it was pretty hard to get enthused about being a grandmother to her baby, even though it was also my son's baby."

• "I'm not comfortable with little babies. Never have been. Now when this boy is big enough to talk to me and I can take him to baseball games, that will be a different story."

• "Becoming a grandparent has made me confront how much my daughter resents the way she was brought up. She's determined to do everything differently from the way I did it. I find it painful."

• "I've gotten used to the peace and quiet and orderliness of a home without children. I find I can't handle the noise, the toys all over the place, the constant strain of having first an infant, now a toddler around. I keep the visits to a minimum."

Parents can be philosophical about grandparents who are uncomfortable with infants but take to older children. The mother of two children, ages seven months and five years, says, "My husband's mother is wonderful with babies, nothing fazes her, she can quiet the fussiest infant. My mom only gets interested later, after a child can talk and is ready for books and games. I know she cares in her own way; it's just who she is."

But when the parents feel that grandparents don't care at all, the disappointment is keen. Even if the relationship has been distant, the birth of a baby seems to bring hope that things may change, along with fantasies about the baby and its loving grandparents. If the grandparents disappoint, the hurt is deep.

"You think you have a good relationship, and then when they are not as involved as you hoped, it really hurts," one mother shared. "My parents live three hours away. They came after the baby was born, but that was it, like they'd done their duty. They didn't even come to the christening, and hardly ever come to see their grandson, maybe once a year. They're too busy with their own lives. My father never even brings a gift when he comes because he says my child has too much already. I feel hurt, but most of all I'm angry—angry for the baby and what he is missing."

"My mother doesn't want to admit she's old enough to be a grandma," says a disappointed son. "She doesn't want to be seen with the baby. She dyes her hair red, wears dresses that are too tight and too short, and thinks she is fooling everyone about her age. I think she's pathetic."

"We had always expected that our parents would play an important role with our children, but after we had triplets, they backed away," says an angry father. "They don't help us at all, just when we need them most. They hardly ever come over—they expect us to come to their house, which is more work than it is worth. I hope I treat my children with more respect when they are adults."

In his book, *Contemporary Grandparenting*, Dr. Arthur Kornhaber calls such grandparental behavior "role dysfunction." Kornhaber, who conducted an in-depth research study on grandparents, found that effective grandparents place a philosophical priority on family life and manage to balance their lives to be able to fulfill and benefit from this role as well as their other diverse roles. "When they do not," Kornhaber writes, "the repercussions of what an adult may rationalize as independent behavior may be perceived as abandonment, even rejection, by children . . . They lose respect for that grandparent."

One of the reasons that some grandparents don't accept their new roles easily is an inability to accept that they are no longer in control. The balance of power has shifted. One grandmother describes it as being "dethroned."

"I see my son's wife raising their son in a way that I don't approve of, without any of the discipline he had growing up, and I can't say anything. My advice is not welcome, even by him. I'm a spectator, without any influence. It's uncomfortable to be around them, so I stay away."

Until this woman can come to terms with the shift in family relations, everyone will lose out. You don't have to approve of the parents to love and enjoy your grandchild. It may be easier to offer to baby-sit in your own home. Parents will appreciate the break, and you can set the rules, so long as they do not come across as criticism of the parents.

Part of the problem in many families is simply that grandparents, particularly grandmothers, do not fit the old definitions. Only her hairdresser knows for sure if today's granny has gray hair, and the cookie jar may be empty, either because Grandma has no time to cook or doesn't want the calories in the house.

Women who used to accept the move from motherhood to

grandmotherhood as a natural progression are now apt to have found new freedom and new interests when their children left home, and may be reluctant to give them up. The middle years from 40 to 60 are a time when many women go back to college and start new careers, rather than sitting around waiting to become grandparents. They feel younger rather than older, but the arrival of grandchildren reminds them that time is marching on, and this can be difficult to accept.

It is a fairly recent development that grandparents can be so busy that their time is at a premium, and it comes just at a time when many parents are overwhelmed by their many responsibilities, as well. When both parents and grandparents have full-time jobs and a tight schedule, just finding time to get together can be a problem. But where there is a will, there is a way to find time for grandchildren. If there is a sincere wish to be in close touch with the baby, it can help to set a special regular date that everyone honors, perhaps a weekend breakfast or one evening each week when everyone eats dinner together—take-out or in a restaurant so nobody has to cook. Or perhaps you can set aside one Saturday each month when you take the baby overnight and give the parents a break.

One executive working grandmother I know now plans her frequent coast-to-coast business trips with a stopover in Denver to visit her children and grandchildren. Since I have the flexibility of working at home, I've given one weekday to baby-sitting for my working daughter and I treat a weekend day as a workday instead. People say to my daughter, "Aren't you lucky?" I feel that I'm the lucky one. I get time to myself with my grandson, a close-up look at his development, and a closeness between us that I would never have any other way.

If you have had problems getting along with your children, the arrival of a baby is an ideal time to try to make amends. People can and do change. You may not be able to resolve longstanding problems, but you can try to put them behind you for the sake of that wonderful grandchild. Whatever was in the past, you now have something new and important in common, and your love for the new baby can draw you closer to the parents. No one can resist another person who loves their baby.

"I said to my son, 'I recognize I didn't do everything right as a parent; I'm going to try to do things better with my grandchildren.'" reported one grandfather. "And he is giving me that chance. My good relationship with my granddaughter has considerably warmed the feeling between me and my son."

"My daughter and I never got along particularly well," says another grandmother. "But when she had the baby, she really appreciated my help and support, and things have gotten so much better."

A baby also presents a chance for closer ties with in-laws. One mother suggests, "My advice is to start improving relationships with your in-law son or daughter before the baby is born. Take your daughter-in-law to lunch. Let her know you are on her team, that you'll try to make life easier for her. Let her set the pace. Give her a gift of a maternity dress and go with her to let her pick it out. Ask her opinion before you choose a baby gift. Invite her friends to a baby shower.

"After the baby is born, bring over frozen casseroles so she doesn't have to cook. Let her go out for a haircut or a class.

Take a class in CPR to show that you will be a safe baby-sitter. If she doesn't seem to want your assistance, give her space. Maybe she is shy and nervous about pleasing you or afraid that you are judging her. Praise can do wonders, and you don't have to be crazy about your daughter-in-law to admire her care of your grandchild.

"It will be better for both of you if you let her set limits on your visits. Encourage her to kick you out when you've over-stayed your welcome."

Sons-in-law can be wooed, as well. Buy the prospective father a book on parenting. Ask to see his baby pictures, and attribute baby's beautiful eyes or good disposition to him. Remember his birthday, and have his favorite foods on hand when he visits.

"Even if you don't like your child's decision on who to marry, you must respect it and treat this person as a parent and an adult," states one young mother. "Look for things you can praise and offer to help. Once you prove that you are a loving grandparent, things will improve."

While grandparenthood may be an unpleasant reminder of age, it can also be the chance to accept your stage of life, to add a new dimension to your life, and to gain new joy. Acknowledging your children as adults and your own changed role is a chance not to grow old, but to grow up.

Whatever it takes to make peace and to find time for family is worth the effort, for to miss out on the joy of grand-parenting is a huge loss to everyone. Dr. Kornhaber's Grandparent Study found that a bond between generations contributes significantly to the health and well-being of both, and helps grandparents as well as grandchildren grow as human beings.

There are few emotions to match the wonder of holding a new baby, and watching a personality blossom. Few feelings in life are so wonderful as the pure and special love that grows between grandchild and grandparent, the gapless generations. Don't let yourself miss out. Listen to the advice of a Missouri grandmother who says, "Love your grandchild . . . it doesn't get any better than this!"

Baby-sitting: How Much Is Too Much?

Taking care of a grandchild can be one of the greatest pleasures of grandparenthood, a chance to relate one-to-one and build closeness, and there is no surer way to endear yourself to parents.

But when and whether to say yes can become a dilemma. Everyone doesn't like baby-sitting, and everyone isn't up to it. Even a small, docile infant requires energy, and an overnight stay means little sleep for grandparents. Once the baby starts getting around, the physical demands go up dramatically. You can't take your eyes off a crawling baby, and chasing a two- or three-year-old round the playground can be exhausting. Lifting a twenty-five-pound child and trying to diaper a wriggling toddler can be hard on even the hardiest grandparent. Even if you set rules at home, your house is not going to remain orderly with a young child around. If parents take for granted that you are always going to be available, you may rightfully feel resentful.

What to do? If you want to do right by everyone, don't play martyr—and don't let baby-sitting become an issue that keeps you away from your family. Decide how much baby-sitting you can comfortably handle, and talk this over frankly with the parents. If short sessions are better for you, say so. If you can't handle an overnight, don't do it. If the parents feel better with a family member around when they go out of town, have them hire a sitter to help you out. You can assure them that you are always ready and willing to assist in an emergency, but asking you to do more than you are physically able isn't fair to you—or to your grandchild.

11

Grand-Sibling Rivalry

"I don't think there was any less sense of wonder when my second granddaughter was born. In fact, this time there was added anticipation because I knew what was coming. Once again, I was able to hold her within an hour of her birth and watch as they weighed and measured her. It was just as wonderful, just as much of a miracle."

You think you'll never love anyone as much as you do that first grandchild. Then lo and behold, here is a newcomer with its own claim on your heart. And make no mistake, that claim is strong. Listen to what grandparents say:

- "Much as I love him, my first grandchild has become an adorable but independent little guy who no longer likes to cuddle. I have to admit, the idea of a new baby to rock and sing to is appealing."

- "This is my first granddaughter and the first girl in our family. There's no question she's special to us."

• "I thought it would be less exciting this time, since it would no longer be new. But this baby is so entirely different. She's so much more social and outgoing. I'm still absolutely crazy about my grandson, but I'm fascinated seeing the differences."

• "I remember rocking and singing to my baby granddaughter when she was the only grandchild and saying to my daughter, 'I don't know if I could love another as much as I love this one.' Then, when my grandson was born, again there was an outpouring of love that I couldn't imagine was possible. I told my granddaughter that the reason we have two sides to our laps is so there is plenty of room for two. And hopefully, if and when there are more, my arms will stretch so far that I can hold them all, with the same abundance of love."

When the new baby is a brother or sister for your first grandchild, parents would like to remind grandparents that it is the older child who needs you most at the start. Even before the baby is born, presents for the prospective big sister or big brother help pave the way. A baby doll with a stroller encourages playing at being Mommy or Daddy, and helps the child identify with caring for a baby. Check the lists on pages 173 and 177 and bring books and videos about new babies.

You may well be called on to look after the older child when Mommy goes to the hospital. Prepare him well in advance and make plans for special things you will do together so he can look forward to your arrival. If you stay on to help the parents, make an extra effort to spend time with the older child, showing that your love hasn't wavered with the arrival of the new infant. There will be moments when he wants his mommy and only his mommy, and that's when you'll get your turn to hold the baby.

When everyone else is sending presents for the new arrival, you can help make the older child feel the benefits of being older with special gifts that only a "big boy" or "big girl" can enjoy, like a new tricycle or wagon.

Plan special outings where the oldest child will still have you all to himself—and have a break from the household that may seem to be revolving around the new baby.

You can also help by being a sounding board, providing an outlet for the negative emotions that are inevitable when a child is forced to share family attention with a newcomer. Ask questions like, "How does it feel to have a baby in the house?" "What do you like about the baby?" "What don't you like about the baby?" If you get negative comments, be understanding. Tell her you know it can be hard to have someone else take up so much of everyone's time, that it is normal to be angry some-times, and assure her that no one is going to be mad at her for sharing her feelings. Remind her that when she was an infant, she required the same kind of attention.

If you are left in charge of both children, keep a keen eye on the older child. Even a loving toddler can hurt an infant by hugging her too hard, over-rocking the cradle, or trying to pick the baby up. Never, never leave the two children alone together.

There is a whole new set of logistics to consider when your

second grandchild belongs to a different son or daughter. Sibling rivalry does not go away when children grow up. Each parent probably thinks his or her children are the most wonderful in the world and secretly wants you to love them best of all.

Lots of factors influence grandparents' feelings about the children of their various children. "I am trying very hard not to favor the first grandchild," one grandmother states. "But it is hard because she lives nearer. Also she is my daughter's child, so I am closer, and her mother asks me for advice more than my daughter-in-law does. And the babies have different personalities. My daughter's child was always so easy to care for, just a little doll. My son's baby was fussy. Baby-sitting was a chore sometimes, and caring for her wasn't easy on them, either. She is seven months old now, so is getting better and more fun to baby-sit. She laughs and plays peekaboo, and I'm sure I'm going to adore her, too, but it is taking longer."

You can't help your feelings any more than your grown children can help feeling a certain amount of normal sibling rivalry, but you can do your best never to let your favoritism show. Here are some do's and don'ts suggested by parents to keep rivalry to a minimum. These same suggestions apply between children in one family as well as among children of various siblings.

• Try to develop a special relationship with each child. You only get to know children well when they have you to themselves, so as much as possible schedule one-to-one time with each grandchild.

• Treat each grandchild as an individual. Don't think you have to do or give equal things to each one. Think of special things to do together that you know will uniquely please each child. Consider each personality, development stage, and interest when you choose gifts. Jane may want a construction toy while Jill would rather have a drawing pad and crayons. How much each costs is not the issue—thoughtfully and genuinely trying to please each child is what matters.

• Don't compare. It's O.K. to note that Cousin Joan likes to sing or Brother Dan likes to build. It's *not* O.K. to say, "I'm surprised you don't like that CD. Cousin Joan liked it," or "You shouldn't throw your blocks. Dan would never do that." The cardinal sin: "Why can't you be more like your brother/sister/cousin?"

• Don't compare parents. Don't tell your working daughter how much more relaxed her stay-at-home sister feels. Don't brag to one son about what a devoted father his brother has become. Siblings who are already rivals will take such comments as criticism and will be resentful.

• Don't brag to parents about the talents or progress of your other grandchildren. Parents may take it as a subtle way of saying the others are somehow better than theirs.

• Give affection equally. Maybe you do have a favorite grandchild (you're only human, after all). But while gifts don't have to match, take special care to give out hugs and kisses and loving words equally to all.

As the family grows, grandparents are prone to have fantasies about one big happy family, where everyone will want to get together regularly and all the cousins will be best friends. Many grandparents plan a vacation for all the children and grandchildren with such idyllic visions before their eyes. Before you fall into this pattern, remember that unless the brothers and sisters are already close, the arrival of a new generation will not change things. Nor are family occasions always what you hope they will be. Childless or unmarried adult children may resent the attention you pay to the younger generation and their parents. Adult brothers and sisters may not approve of each other's parenting techniques. Babies cry, toddlers hit each other, brothers and sisters fight. If you can remember the family get-togethers where you and your spouse recounted horror stories of the day when you were safely behind closed doors at night, you will sympathize with the fact that your children will be no different. Does this mean you shouldn't get together? Not at all. The plusses outweigh the problems in most families. But do plan these reunions with realistic expectations—and don't overdo the time spent together.

Like all our major roles in life, becoming a grandparent is a learning experience. Some of the learning may be difficult. It isn't easy to find that your views are not always relevant, that you are not up on new techniques, that you must sit back and let your children assume their roles as parents as they see fit.

As a reward, you may find that as time goes by you are more appreciated as a parent. I read a message on the Internet called "I'm becoming my mother," with the story of a young mother who says she and her siblings hated a humming sound their mother used to quiet them when they were little. Now she finds herself using it on her own children. A daughter I know remembers how she bristled when her mother called the children by each other's names—but understands, now that she finds herself doing the same thing. "I understand lots of things about my mother now—and I appreciate her more than I ever did before," she says.

Greater understanding between grandparents and their adult children as they see each other in new roles, a deep unconditional love for the next generation, and a new zest for living from being with the young are some of the wonderful benefits that make the challenges of grandparenting worthwhile.

Giving equivalent love and attention to several grandchildren is one of the challenges. It takes effort and care. Your first grandchild will naturally mind that he can no longer have all of your time. But you can explain that while they may have to share their time, grandparents never have to divide their love—it just grows bigger to make room for everyone.

The Family Book

A project guaranteed to enthrall youngsters age three and up is a family book created by their grandparents. Make an album tracing the family's history. You can buy albums called "Grandmother Remembers" or "Grandfather Remembers" to guide your efforts, but an ordinary photo album serves just as well. Start with yourselves growing up, including your own parents. Follow your family from the time you married to the birth of your own children, and continue right up to the present, including grandchildren. You can keep adding to the album as new arrivals join the family.

Intersperse the pictures with tapes or written stories with your memories of the past. As they grow older, children are fascinated by learning about their grandparents' past, because it is their own past, as well. Looking at pictures together is a great way to begin. You'll be creating a family history that will let your grandchildren know you better, and will be treasured by your children, as well.

part 2

Buying for Baby

Buying the Basics

Overheard at a crafts fair: Husband: "That's pretty. Do you want to try it on?" Wife: "First, let's take care of the grandchildren."

With all the differences in childbirth, one thing never seems to change: most prospective grandparents can't wait to go shopping for the baby. Along with getting a head start on fun stuff like cute outfits and cuddly teddy bears, if you are able, you'll probably want to give the parents a hand with some of the bigger purchases.

They are no doubt reading up on and asking their own experienced friends about the best products. If you want to give them a helpful book (or do some reading for yourself), there are several comprehensive buying guides. The *Guide to Baby Products* published by Consumer Reports Books gives their familiar brand-name ratings, safety guides, and recommendations for everything from diapers to portable cribs. *The Childwise Catalog* by Jack Gillis and Mary Ellen R. Fise is published by the Consumer Federation of America and gives spe-

139

cific brand and name recommendations for products and toys as well as lists of products that have had safety recalls. *Baby Stuff* is written by Ari Lipper, who has been selling baby products for many years, knows what he is talking about, and gives good advice and specific buying recommendations in all price ranges. (See pages 185–86 for more information on these titles.)

The first gifts for baby come with the tried-and-true custom of baby showers. Don't do your gift buying before the shower because it can do a lot to help fill the new family's needs. Friends and coworkers often go in together to buy big things like strollers, and fewer layette items may be needed after pals and relatives pitch in.

When you are choosing your own shower gifts, don't forget presents for the future mom. A good, sturdy diaper bag is one possibility; one handy model recommended by some mothers can be worn several ways—as a backpack, shoulder bag, or handbag. Another working mother suggests getting a conservative bag like those offered by the Lands' End catalog (see page 181) rather than one with cutesy patterns all over it. "It looks much better when I have to take the baby into the office with me," she explains.

A new bed jacket for the hospital and a baby book to keep track of important milestones are other welcome gifts. Another mother appreciated receiving books on parenting to add to her library.

Another more expensive idea is a comfy, well-padded glider rocker for nursing the baby. Mothers say these are the greatest, better than traditional rockers. Try to get one with an ottoman or footrest. If the family does not already own a portable phone, they will bless you for this gift.

THE BASICS

The crib and furniture for baby's room, a stroller, and a car seat are the basic necessities for new babies. These important items should be chosen by the parents even if you pay for them, but that doesn't mean you can't have fun shopping around and looking at the new options. Clever cribs these days, for example, can convert into toddler beds and then full-size beds. They come with names like Cribs 4 Life and Crib to College.

One whimsical source of clever plywood furniture is a company called Leap Frog. They make items such as Topsy Turvy, a high chair that can become a booster seat or, turned upside down, a fanciful throne for an older child. Other products include a cradle-cum-teeter-totter called Cat's Cradle, and a worktable called Hide and Seek with hidden storage and a fold-out blackboard. Phone (203) 254-7134 for a catalog.

Don't buy anything major until you consult with parents. You don't want your children to feel like the mother who stated, "My mother-in-law was obsessed with the baby. When I was pregnant she bought everything, including the crib. I didn't even get to pick it out. She then arranged the room and picked the theme. Some people thought that I was crazy for getting mad, but it was an invasion on my rightful territory. When she started to refer to 'my baby,' I finally lost it. I told her, 'I appreciate everything that you have done, but enough is enough. Just because you bought all the baby's things does not entitle you to this baby! If you feel that way maybe you should take the things back and have your own baby!' She's been a lot calmer since then."

Consult the parents before you buy anything—and don't be insulted if your taste doesn't match theirs. Be sure anything you buy is returnable. If the parents live in another city, you may have to content yourself with sending a check.

If you've been looking around at other babies since you heard your own good news, you'll see that few couples have fancy carriages like those their mothers might have used. The most popular choice today is a soft-sided combination carriage-stroller, with adjustable seats so that the baby can lie back or sit up. Reversible handles switch from carriage to stroller position. The status names are Peg Perego, McLaren, and Aprica. The best lower-priced strollers are made by Graco and Century.

Carriage-strollers can cost anywhere from $100 to $400. Before you go for the top of the line, remember that many parents change to a lighter weight stroller as soon as the baby can sit up. The heavier the stroller, the harder it is to push a growing youngster. Many of these are known as umbrella strollers because they are easy to fold up; the best ones can be folded with one hand while baby is held in the other.

Stroller extras to look for are a removable, washable liner and a rain cover. If possible, have the mother-to-be push the stroller to be sure that the handle is at a comfortable height. Also be sure that the wheels swivel and turn easily.

Remember those cute little car seats with steering wheels attached that we hung over the front seat of the car? When you see the new car seats for babies, you'll wonder how your kids ever survived to adulthood riding in them. The only safety belt I remember was a thin plastic strap. Nowadays, babies ride in the backseat, securely strapped into permanently attached seats, the best of which have five-way straps. It may take you many tries to figure out how to work those straps; one grandmother told me the hardest thing she had to learn was how to get the baby out of the car seat!

Many infant car seats can be lifted out and used as a baby carrier. You can also buy car seat carriage frames, a welcome gift since toting the seat becomes a heavy load as the baby grows bigger.

There are stringent safety regulations for car seats, as well as strollers and cribs; if you do happen to be buying these on your own, read the tags and consult some of the buying guides on page 185 to be sure they comply with the Consumer Products Safety Commission standards.

THE LAYETTE

In case you've forgotten, the basic layette consists of infant clothes and accessories Mother will want to have on hand when the baby first comes home. Most mothers advise against buying more than a couple of items in newborn sizes because they are outgrown so quickly. Better to roll up the sleeves and have things a little baggy at the start.

As to how many of each item to buy, every list seems to give a different number. The numbers here are a consensus of what mothers recommend as a start; you can always add more later if necessary. If the parents have their own washing machine, they may be able to get along with less. Here are the layette basics:

Six receiving blankets

Thin, soft cotton blankets, usually 36 inches square, that are used to swaddle infants, and double as lightweight blankets for crib or carriage.

Six knitted shirts

The most popular version is the "Onesie," a one-piece stretchy T-shirt with a snap bottom. Since they snap over the diaper, they don't ride up. Some parents prefer shirts that snap on the side, because you don't have to pull them over the baby's head. These are especially useful when the baby first comes home, before the umbilical cord has fallen off, since they are loose and won't press on the cord.

Six stretchys

One-piece stretch outfits with snaps running down the front and one leg. This is the basic "uniform" for infants, neatly covering all the parts and keeping baby warm. In flame-retardant fabric with feet, they double as pajamas.

Gowns

These are optional, but some mothers prefer them to stretchys because you don't have to push the baby's feet into separate legs. They can be tightened at the bottom for warmth, but there's plenty of room for kicking.

Twelve cloth diapers

Even if the parents are planning to use disposable diapers, a dozen cloth diapers are needed to go across the shoulder for burping baby and to lie under baby's face in the crib to catch drool.

Four booties

The most practical choices are tiny cotton socks with an elastic band that keeps them from slipping off.

Bath supplies

Two each, soft hooded towels and baby washcloths. A plastic tub to go into the big bathtub will be useful eventually; at the start, many families use the kitchen sink, which is a lot more comfortable for moms than bending over the tub.

Crib supplies

Waterproof sheet, two quilted pads, two crib sheets, two blankets, crib bumper. You may be shocked when you see the price of bumpers—they can go up as high as $200! It's imperative to consult the parents-to-be before buying bumpers—they should go with the color scheme and room decor.

GRANDPARENT GOODIES

Parents will buy or borrow the necessities with or without you, but you may be able to supply some extras they'll welcome. Here are the most useful gifts most of the parents polled recommend:

Baby monitor

A set consisting of a microphone in baby's room and a portable speaker that lets you hear the baby while you are in another room. Most work either on batteries or an AC adapter. Monitors cost from $35 to $70; if you've hit the lottery and want to spend $350 or more, you can go for a video monitor so the parents can keep watch over the baby.

Infant seat

Also known as a "bouncy seat," these are made of fabric stretched over a bouncy wire frame with a removable toy bar across the front. At the start, this is simply a semireclining seat with good support for baby, and a handy place to feed her when she starts getting solid foods. As she gets older, she'll enjoy playing with the toy bar and will soon discover that bouncing is fun. Most parents say this is a necessity for the first six months or until the baby can sit alone. They cost $40 to $60. Some parents just love the Fisher-Price bouncer seat with a button on the front that makes the seat vibrate, almost like the motion of a car and almost as good for putting baby to sleep. One mother highly recommends the Fisher-Price Cradle Rocker Seat, an infant seat that turns into a rocker or cradle.

Mobile for the crib

Babies are developing right from the time of birth, and mobiles provide important stimulation. The Right Start catalog offers a clever version with a changing series of attachable cards that includes a set in black and white, the colors youngest babies see best. It costs about $19.95.

Crib vibrator

Far from essential, but maybe worth the investment if the gentle motion helps get a fussy baby to sleep.

Portable crib

The most popular and most easily portable crib is made of aluminum tubing with nylon mesh sides. In most young families, it does occasional double duty as a playpen. It is made in one piece, collapses to a very compact size, and comes with its own nylon bag, so parents can easily put it in the car or even take it on a plane when they come to visit Grandma and Grandpa. Graco's "Pack 'n Play" is a popular choice and a long-term piece of equipment praised by both parents and grandparents. It costs around $100.

Bassinet or cradle

These are luxuries because they are used for such a short time, typically only three months, but during those first few months, it can be very handy to have a small, portable sleeper that lets parents keep the baby close at hand. Bassinets are basically lined baskets, usually on wheels; they can cost $40 to $100. Cradles are slightly larger and less portable, but they allow you to rock a restless baby to sleep. You pay a lot for this added pleasure, however—cradles run $130 to $500. One Step Ahead offers a cradle that later converts to a gliding swing chair for $150. Some people believe that a newborn feels more secure in a bassinet or cradle for the first few weeks. There's no scientific proof of this, but they do seem to be cozier quarters for a wee infant.

Baby swing

Motorized swings, which run on batteries (get rechargeables), are a pure luxury, but babies do love them and parents do, too, especially when they keep the baby occupied long enough to have a peaceful dinner or lull the little darling to sleep. Swings should have stable legs and come with padded seats and safety bars, so that tots can stay safe as well as happy. The cost is from $60 to $125.

Jumper seat

These are bouncy seats that hook on to a doorway and keep baby happy and in view. They hang on springs so baby can bounce, and can be adjusted in height as the baby grows so toes just clear the floor. Some parents were concerned about the safety of the suspended seats, but others absolutely swear by them. One family hangs them in the kitchen to keep the bouncing baby happy while Mom or Dad makes dinner; one mother reports she hung hers on the bathroom door so she could take a quick shower. Jumpers can be used from the time the baby holds his head up until he walks. They cost from $20 to $35. The better ones have a plastic frame to support the baby and molding on the sides to protect the doorway. Before you buy, be sure the doorways of baby's home meet the requirements for a jumper—the wall must be between three and six inches thick, the molding must be at least a half-inch wide and firmly attached.

Car seat carriage frame

No need to wake baby to move her from the car seat to the stroller with one of these. Just lift out the seat and place it on a car seat carriage frame. For $40, you can buy a folding frame made to hold all of the most popular car seat models.

Umbrella stroller

Lighter and more portable, the umbrella stroller is essential for city mothers getting on and off buses. My suburban daughter keeps hers in the trunk of her car, uses it when she goes shopping or visiting, and leaves it with me when the baby visits. Umbrella strollers cost anywhere from $29 to $225; more expensive models have reclining seat backs, provide a footrest, and have swiveling wheels that make them easier to steer. Depending on whether the seat reclines, umbrella strollers are suitable for babies beginning at three or six months and, as noted, they are so much easier to push that most mothers quickly favor them over the more expensive, heavier strollers.

Jogging stroller

If Mommy-to-be and/or Daddy-to-be are runners, they'll love this three-wheel stroller that you can push ahead of you while you run. It will set you back about $150.

Carriers

These slinglike, soft baby seats made of sturdy cloth can hold the baby against you in front or be used as a backpack. Some parents say they are not comfortable and were seldom used, others love them. A mother of a colicky baby said that carrying her infant in a front sling quieted and comforted him.

Video camera

They'll bless you for this one—and if you live far from the baby it will be a gift to yourself as well as the parents, allowing you to share the baby's progress.

Mini food processor

This will be welcomed by parents who plan to make their own baby food. It allows them to create pureed food for baby from small portions of whatever they are eating for dinner.

Toy chest

It will be needed as the toys begin to accumulate, which will be soon. Toy storage benches do double duty as seats. Be sure to choose a chest with a safe lid that stays up until firmly pushed down. Pier 1 has some enchanting toy chest designs; they cost about $135.

"Head rolls"

These are little pillows that fit around the back of the neck and prop a newborn's head in the car seat.

If you're looking for more unusual little goodies, check the catalogs. One Step Ahead offers a musical night-light; tapes of lullabies; a soft, flexible activity arch with toys that hang over the crib; and a car seat that lifts out as a carrier and also attaches to a swing frame.

The Right Start catalog features a 3-D Activity Gym for infants for $44.95. Baby lies on a soft mat spanned by a padded arch. Dangling from the arch are soft, safe toys to look at and reach for. It all folds and fits into a carrying bag for travel.

Cloth and terry bibs may be cute, but mothers say they get stained in no time, and if you try to bleach them, the designs fade out. Look for a vinyl fabric with a pocket to catch spills. The best bibs I've seen, aptly named "Super Bibs," are in the First Step catalog. They have handy Velcro closings, and the vinyl fabric is almost indestructible. They're still going strong in our family after three years. Three bibs cost $14.95.

What Ever Happened To . . .

A lot of the baby equipment you remember isn't around anymore—or isn't used very much. Here are some of the disappearances large and small noted by grandparents:

- **Diaper pins.** Nobody misses them now that Velcro is around and you never have to worry about sticking baby. Even when cloth diapers are used, they can be folded inside rubber pants with Velcro closings.

- **Square diapers.** No more folding diapers into triangles. Cloth diapers these days come in rectangular shapes with sensible extra padding in the middle, where it is most needed. They adjust to fit the baby's length by being folded down at the top.

- **Sterilizers.** Families with dishwashers no longer have to boil those bottles every day.

- **Wooden playpens.** You may have found them indispensable, but chances are your children will use their portable playpen/crib if they use anything at all—many parents think playpens are too confining. One variation that is more acceptable to some parents is an activity yard made of plastic panels that can be assembled into a circle or octagon shape. These give the baby much more room to roam.

- **Changing tables.** These are still around in the stores, but most mothers say they are a waste of money, that you can do just as well with inexpensive pads that fit on the top of a dresser.

- **Walkers.** Walkers haven't disappeared, either, but lots of parents discourage them because they can be unsafe. Instead, they recommend "Exersaucers," which are essentially walkers without wheels. They allow the baby to bounce and swivel and exercise, but not to careen into furniture or down the stairs.

All About Toys

"Children usually love simple toys best and play with them longest."

—Dr. Benjamin Spock

When you buy toys for your grandchildren, you are giving more than fun. It has been said that play is work for young children, the way that they learn and grow, physically, mentally, and socially. Toys are the tools that enable them to work well.

According to a guide published by the U.S. Consumer Product Safety Commission in cooperation with developmental and educational psychologists, young children need five types of play for well-rounded development:

• Manipulative play that increases hand/eye coordination. At the start, this means toys to look at, touch, and reach for. Later on, blocks, nesting and stacking toys, shape sorters, and miniature cars and trucks are favorites.

• Active play that exercises muscles, such as outdoor play equipment, balls and sports equipment, push toys, ride-on cars and tricycles.

• Creative play such as crayons, paints, and music.

• Learning play such as books and games.

• Make-believe play that stimulates the imagination, such as dolls, stuffed toys, and puppets.

Two basic toys recommended for grandparents to give and to have on hand for little visitors serve several purposes.

Balls

Balls are versatile toys that are enjoyed from infant days right through toddler years. Textured balls are for the youngest; later baby enjoys soft squeeze balls. Balls of all sizes are good for rolling and chasing and later for throwing, kicking, and catching.

One of the most enduring gifts anyone gave to my grandson was a set of three Fun Balls sold at Gymboree stores for about $6. These clever hollow plastic balls are lightweight and covered with smooth holes that make them easy for babies to grasp. They can be used outdoors as well as inside, since they go into the dishwasher. They are fun in a sandbox, where the sand dribbles out of the holes, and in the bathtub, where they float and water runs out of the holes when they are submerged. Each ball is a different color, so they also help teach color identification.

Blocks

Babies like to touch and hold soft blocks made of cloth. Later on a good set of wooden building blocks is a basic that helps build coordination and stimulate the imagination.

It is "politically correct" these days to be sure that little boys have dolls and girls have their share of cars and trucks, but mothers report that some differences in the sexes seem ingrained no matter how equal the opportunity. You'll still notice that by age two, girls will gravitate to dressing and caring for dolls while boys like manipulating trains and cars.

The charts here suggest other toys that are appropriate in each group for babies and toddlers. Like all charts using ages, these are arbitrary and meant as a general guide. Your grandchild may not stack blocks or use crayons according to a timetable any more than he will walk or talk on someone else's schedule, but rest assured he'll get to everything in his own time.

Age recommendations on toy packages are helpful up to a point, but you should always choose toys that are appropriate for a particular child's present abilities, rather than buying something that will only prove frustrating. Don't rush to buy the fanciest toys, especially those that require batteries. My grandson spends far more time with the simple wooden toy train and track he controls himself than with a fancy battery-run train with remote control that he received as a gift.

NEWBORN TO TWO MONTHS

Toys for the first two months are for looking and listening. Even young infants enjoy hearing music and enjoy a variety of things to look at. In the early weeks, while sight is still developing, the objects infants see best are those with high contrast, such as black-and-white designs. They like to look at simple designs and human features, especially eyes. Good choices:

- Black-and-white mobiles to hang over the crib

- Soft toys with different textures

- Music boxes, lullaby tapes, and CDs

- Mirrors that can be fastened to the side of a crib or playpen

TWO MONTHS TO SIX MONTHS

As infants develop, they become more than spectators, moving on to sucking, biting, touching, batting, and grasping. Babies explore objects by mouthing them, so it is important that their toys be unbreakable, have no sharp points or edges, and have no small pieces that could be swallowed. Be sure to check labels for age-appropriateness. One-piece toys are the best choices. Avoid balls made of foam—small pieces may be bitten off and swallowed. Children at this stage enjoy:

- Simple rattles

- Teething toys

- Squeeze and squeak toys

- Textured balls

- Crib gyms

- Activity quilts

- Floor gyms

- Busy boxes

- Plastic keys on ring

AGES SEVEN MONTHS TO ONE YEAR

As baby learns to sit alone and begins to creep, crawl, and stand, there is increased interest in moving around and practicing motor skills. Toys that can be opened and shut and emptied and filled become favorites, along with the first nesting and stacking toys.

Babies tend to get lots of stuffed animals that are too big for them to handle; small ones with arms and legs that they can grasp easily in one hand are favorites. Moms will thank you if the animals are washable.

Kids at this age like to press buttons, turn things, and push balls and toys on wheels. They love toys that make music, especially when they can activate the music by themselves. There are many kinds of miniature pianos that play a song at the touch of a key, and Disney's Melody-Go-Round is a ball that plays music when it is tipped by the baby.

Older babies like toy cars, but look for sturdy ones without parts that can come off and go into the mouth. Save the fancy model cars for later.

Other recommended toys include:

- Soft blocks

- Toys on suction cups for the high chair tray

- Squeeze toys

- Roly-poly wobbling toys

- Activity boxes

- Stacking rings

- Floating toys for the bath

- Filling and spilling toys

- Sturdy push toys for beginning walkers

ONE TO ONE-AND-A-HALF-YEAR-OLDS

From around age one on, sit-on wheeled toys that children can propel with their feet are important ways to exercise muscles, and to gain the satisfaction of being able to move by themselves even before they can walk. Simple ride-ons in the shape of cars and trucks are favorites. A ride-on with a handle in back does double duty as a push toy. Look for ride-ons that are sturdy and low to the ground, with wide seats so that children can get on and off by themselves. A horn and a storage bin under the seat make for extra fun.

Once the baby is walking, push toys like corn poppers, doll carriages, or miniature shopping carts are favorites, as are pull toys with strings. Choose pull toys with sturdy bases that don't tip over easily. Look for toys that make sounds, whether it's the clacking wheels of a toy school bus, or a jack-in-the-box (with adult supervision). Stuffed animals with sound effects are also favorites; just be sure the sound box is sewn safely inside.

Children continue to love musical toys that allow them to play a tune at the touch of a button, as well as toys that spin or move with controls simple enough so they can work them on their own.

Play scenes like a miniature farm or a garage are of interest now mostly for handling the figures, so wait awhile. Instead of buying a farm with a fancy price tag, look for an inexpensive set of small farm animals.

Best suggestions for this age:

• Push and pull toys

• Action toys simple enough for baby to make things happen, i.e., push a button to make things spin or make balls pop up

• Pounding/hammering toys

- Dolls, doll beds, and carriages

- Toy telephones

- Toy cameras

- Musical toys

- Spinning toys easy enough for toddlers to work themselves

AGES ONE-AND-A-HALF TO TWO

Blocks are of increasing interest now, though as much for knocking down as building up. Outdoor equipment provides important exercise and makes for great gifts. First climbers and junior gyms can go indoors or out, and cost from $80 to $100. Wading pools and sandboxes are great for children with backyards.

Other appropriate choices:

- Child-size table and chairs

- Simple tape players and toy CD players that the child can turn on himself (You'll still have to load it for a while)

- Rhythm instruments like maracas that are operated by shaking

- Shape sorters

- Fill and dump toys

- Sturdy cars

• Dolls

• Beginner wooden puzzles with knobs on the pieces for easy handling

TWO- TO THREE-YEAR-OLDS

Around age two, you can work up to a "convertible" tricycle that will grow with the child, letting him continue to move by pushing his feet, but also with pedals. A tall push handle lets you give a ride while toddlers rest their feet on the pedals and learn the motion, and before long he will take off on his own, much to his delight.

Children now are learning to kick, throw, and catch, so a large bouncy ball is in order. As finger dexterity improves, a child is able to work with slightly more complex wooden puzzles and, with your supervision, to scribble with large beginner crayons and cut out shapes with play dough. By around three they are beginning to learn to manipulate buttons. They like to imitate adult tasks like cooking or mowing the lawn, and are beginning to make one toy carry out actions on other toys. Favorite toys include:

• Sets of many small objects—little people, animals

• Toys that move or can be moved and manipulated, cars, trucks, etc.

• Sorting toys

- Small wagons

- Small light wheelbarrow

- Push toys that look like adult equipment, such as a lawn mower, rake and hoe, snow shovel

- Magnetic boards with letters, numbers, shapes, animals, people

- Duplo large blocks

- Simple wooden train and track

- Toys for lacing, buttoning, snapping, hooking

- Sandbox toys

- Dolls and doll-care accessories such as a bottle or blanket

- Small hand puppets

- Xylophones

- Lotto matching games based on color pictures

- Play scenes—garages and farms by now are more meaningful, and can keep children happily occupied for long periods

- Videotapes, tapes, CDs (to be operated by adults)

AGES THREE TO FOUR

Somewhere around age three, the child will gain enough coordination and muscle power to pedal on a regular tricycle, which will be a favorite usually to age five, when it is time for a two-wheeler with training wheels.

The better their dexterity, the more interested children become in building, so simple construction toys can be added to blocks. Children are now increasingly drawn to more realistic toys, such as dolls with hair and moving eyes and jazzy racing cars. Pretend play is big at this stage, so miniature kitchen equipment is a great grandparent gift, along with a puppet stage and simple puppets. Toys that help teach matching, sorting, shapes, colors, numbers, and letters are appropriate now. Other useful choices:

- Small wagons and wheelbarrows (still favorites)

- Interlocking building sets (Duplo, Lego)

- Age-appropriate puzzles (age three, up to 20 pieces)

- Number and letter puzzles, puzzle clocks

- Color Forms

- Kick balls

- Matching and sorting toys

- Simple counting toys

- Lacing and stringing toys

- Realistic dolls

- Simple puppets, puppet stage

- Music boxes and other music-making toys

- Horns, whistles, simple recorder

- Crayons, paints, Magic Markers (be sure they are washable)

- Toy stethoscope

- Matchbox cars, roadways with ramps

- Chalkboards and chalk

- Picture bingo

- Jumbo dominoes

- Action-adventure figures

- First simple dollhouse

- More complex train track setups

- Easels, brushes, and washable paints

- Sticker books

- Toy dishes

- Candyland game

PARENT PICKS

Parents almost unanimously asked for toys that allow the child to use his imagination, one big reason that blocks are a top choice. Other toys they picked as favorites:

BIRTH TO AGE ONE

- Colorfun Ball, Gund

- Fun Balls, Gymboree

- Roll 'n Rattle Ball, Playskool

- Balls in a Bowl, *Parents Magazine* Toys (*Parents Magazine* has a "toy of the month" option that makes a great gift.)

- Stacking Clown, Little Tikes

- Sesame Street Grow 'n Go Activity Wagon, Tyco

- Soft Picture Blocks, Constructive Playthings

- Lights 'n Sound Piano, Fisher-Price

- Melody-Go-Round, Disney

AGES ONE TO TWO

- Cozy Coupe by Little Tikes, a ride-in toy car that one mother calls "the BMW of the toddler set"

- Weeble Fire Station Ride-on, Playskool

- Easy-Touch Tape Player, Mattel

- Musical Boom Box, Fisher-Price

- Corn Popper, Fisher-Price

- Fisher-Price School Bus

- Fisher-Price Pullalong Telephone

- Sesame Street dolls, Playskool (Pick your child's favorite—Big Bird, Elmo, Cookie Monster, Bert, or Ernie)

- Sesame Street Melody Pals, Tyco (press the bellies to hear a tune)

- Sesame Street Tub Sub, Tyco

- Play Slide, Little Tikes

AGES TWO TO THREE

- Duplo Blocks

- Lego Blocks

- Play-Doh Fun Factory

- Little People Garage, Fisher-Price

- Little People Farm, Fisher-Price

- Washable So-Big Crayons, Crayola

• Brio and Thomas the Tank Engine tracks and trains (the tracks are interchangeable)

Tips on Picking Backyard Gym Sets

• Look for more than swings and slides—climbing ladders and bars are important for developing muscles and imagination.

• Be sure construction is sturdy; don't buy a set unless you can see it set up.

• Choose a scale that is appropriate for preschoolers; trying to use equipment meant for older children can lead to frustration and accidents.

• Avoid sets with rough or sharp edges; be sure nuts and bolts are placed where they won't snag clothes.

• Check the weight capacity; be sure two or three children can safely play together.

Books, Music, and Videos for Baby

"I never feel so close to my grandchild as when we are snuggled together, sharing a book."

There is no greater gift you can give your grandchild than a love for books. From the earliest age, reading is a chance for a child to nestle close in your lap, to share sights and hear sounds that will later turn into words. Toddlers learn about the world in a much more personal way by reading rather than by watching even the most educational television shows because there is always an adult to share, explain, answer questions, and relate what is being read to the child's world. In families where busy working parents have limited time for reading, grandparents can fill an important need.

Be prepared: young ones like hearing the same story over and over until it is so familiar that they will begin filling in the words themselves. These are the building blocks to word recognition that will one day enable your grandchild to read for himself.

While everything else may be changing, when you go to the bookstore you'll be happy to see that the classics you read to your own very young children are still the best around. The only change is that favorites like *Goodnight Moon*, a perennial since 1947, are now available in sturdy cardboard versions with pages little fingers can turn by themselves without tearing.

What to look for for the very young? Little ones like books with clear, bright pictures; short text; and simple stories about familiar subjects. They like hearing the cadence of rhymes and, as they get a bit older, they love books with things to touch and to manipulate. There's still no better beginner book than *Pat the Bunny*, a best-seller for over 40 years. Pop-up books, hidden picture books, and books with a surprise on each page are fun for toddlers.

Stories with repetition are favorites, especially stories about animals, when they give the child a chance to fill in sounds like "moo," "oink," and "quack."

Little children are fond of small-format cardboard books that fit small hands. Anything by Jan Pienkowski or Dick Bruna is almost sure to please with their bright graphics and simple text, and they teach a bit by showing appealing pictures of shapes, letters, or numbers.

Introducing letter and number books may be valuable learning tools, but always use them as a game, not as a serious attempt to teach. William Wegman's books spelling out letters and numbers with photos of his amazing dogs delight both children and grown-ups.

When you are looking for picture books for toddlers, a sure sign of a winner is the gold seal on the cover that signifies a

Caldecott Medal award. These prizes go to the artist or illustrator of the best American picture book of the year.

Authors whose picture books are almost guaranteed to please are Eric Carle, Crockett Johnson, and Margaret Wise Brown.

Once children are old enough to understand the meaning of what you are reading, they love silly humor. By age three information books on dinosaurs or nature are of interest. Look for books about shells, stars, birds, trees, and animals. In fact, you can help your grandchild make a book by finding pictures of animals or flowers in magazines.

Here are some of the books that parents and grandparents recommend wholeheartedly:

CLASSICS FOR BABIES AND YOUNG TODDLERS

Baby Animal Friends by Phoebe Dunn

Barnyard Banter by Denise Fleming

The Carrot Seed by Ruth Kraus, illustrations by Crockett Johnson

Goodnight Moon by Margaret Wise Brown

Horns to Toes by Sandra Boynton

Jamberry by Bruce Degen

Pat the Bunny by Dorothy Kunhardt

Spot's Toys, Where's Spot?, Spot Looks at Colors, and other Spot books by Eric Hill

Tomie's Little Mother Goose by Tomie dePaola

AGES ONE TO TWO

A Child's Good Night Book by Margaret Wise Brown

A Is for Angry by Sandra Boynton

The Big Red Barn by Margaret Wise Brown

Brown Bear, Brown Bear, What Do You See? by Bill Martin, Jr., and Eric Carle

Harold and the Purple Crayon by Crockett Johnson

My First Look at . . . series, including *Numbers, Shapes, Sizes,* published by Random House

One Two Three by William Wegman

Polar Bear, Polar Bear, What Do You Hear? by Bill Martin, Jr., and Eric Carle

The Runaway Bunny by Margaret Wise Brown

The Snowy Day by Ezra Jack Keats

Triangle, Square, Circle by William Wegman

The Very Busy Spider by Eric Carle

The Very Hungry Caterpillar by Eric Carle

AGES TWO TO THREE

Bedtime for Francis by Tana Hoban

Blueberries for Sal by Robert McCloskey

Little Bear stories by Maurice Sendak

The Little Engine That Could by Watty Piper

Make Way for Ducklings by Robert McCloskey

AGES THREE TO FOUR

Caps for Sale by Esphyr Slobodkina

Curious George by H. A. Rey

Guess How Much I Love You by Sam McBratney

Millions of Cats by Wanda Gag

The Tale of Peter Rabbit by Beatrix Potter

The Velveteen Rabbit by Margery Williams

The Very Lonely Firefly by Eric Carle

The Very Quiet Cricket by Eric Carle

Where's Bunny's Mommy by Charlotte Doyle

Where the Wild Things Are by Maurice Sendak

BOOKS TO HELP PREPARE FOR A NEW BABY

Darcy and Gran Don't Like Babies by Jane Cutler

When the New Baby Comes I'm Moving Out by Martha Alexander

When You Were a Baby Blue Chip by Ann Jonas

ZaZa's Baby Brother by Lucy Cousins

Beginner reader books make excellent read-alouds for toddlers of all ages for their colorful pictures and short, simple text. You can't go wrong with Dr. Seuss rhyming books such as:

The Cat in the Hat

Dr. Seuss' ABC

Green Eggs and Ham

If I Ran the Zoo
One Fish, Two Fish

Other recommendations:
Happy Birthday Thomas, based on The Railway Series by Rev. W. Awdry
Put Me in the Zoo by Robert Lopshire
Are You My Mother? by P. D. Eastman

TAPES AND COMPACT DISCS
FOR YOUNG CHILDREN

Music should be part of every young child's life. At the start, calming lullabies will soothe the baby to sleep. Then you can buy your grandchild a tape recorder and watch the fun as she dances around and quickly learns the words.

Many pop stars have made children's albums that parents and grandparents can also enjoy. And you don't always have to stick with selections for children. By age two and a half, my grandson knew his parents' Willie Nelson recording by heart.

If you can't find them in your local stores, all of the tapes and videos to follow can be ordered from Alcazar Music, listed on page 184.

The following are parents' recommendations:

Baby's Bedtime by Judy Collins, Lightyear
Bananaphone by Raffi, MCA
Barney's Favorites, Lyons (Parents don't always love Barney, but kids do; this is one of many Barney tapes.)

A Cathy & Marcy Collection for Kids by Cathy Fink & Marcy Marxer, Rounder

A Child's Celebration of Song, Music for Little People

A Child's Gift of Lullabies, Someday Baby, Inc.

The Classical Child, Metro Music

Family & Friends by Joanie Bartels, Discovery Music

Hand in Hand, with Joni Mitchell, John Lennon, Jackson Browne, Bobby McFerrin, The Pretenders, Kenny Loggins, and others, Music for Little People

Magic series by Joanie Bartels: *Lullaby Magic, Bathtime Magic, Morning Magic, Silly Time Magic, Simply Magic, Travelin' Magic*; Discovery Music

Nobody Else Like Me by Cathy Fink & Marcy Marxer, Community Music, Inc.

Peter, Paul & Mommy, Too, by Peter, Paul & Mary, Warner Brothers

Pete Seeger's Family Concert, Sony Wonder

Return to Pooh Corner by Kenny Loggins, Sony Wonder

Sesame Street, Silly Songs, Sony Wonder (or dozens of other *Sesame Street* tapes and CDs that fans of the show will love, some with accompanying books, all on Sony Wonder)

Singable Songs for the Very Young by Raffi, MCA

If your grandchild is colicky, you'll be blessed if you give the parents *Grandma's Colic Cure*, a CD featuring white noise from vacuum, hair dryer, clothes dryer, etc., with names like "The Hoover Hustle" and "Someone to Wash Over Me." (See page 33 for the origin of this tape.) It can be ordered from Two Sisters

Productions, P.O. Box 29362, Richmond, VA 23242 for $11.95 plus $2 handling fee.

VIDEOS

This being a visual age, your grandchildren are probably going to watch television. You can help make sure this is a positive experience by giving (and stocking up on) good videos. Some of the possibilities:

FAVORITE BOOKS NOW IN VIDEO FORM

These shouldn't replace the books, but may help keep youngsters occupied on a cranky or rainy day.

Babar series (age three and up), Family Home Entertainment
Dr. Seuss series: *Green Eggs and Ham, Horton Hatches the Egg*, and many others, Sony Wonder Video
Ezra Jack Keats Library, Children's Circle Video
Harold and the Purple Crayon and other Harold Stories, Children's Circle Video
Madeline series, narrated by Christopher Plummer (age three and up), Golden Book Video
Richard Scarry series: *Best Busy People Video Ever, Best Sing Along Mother Goose Video Ever, Best Silly Stories and Songs Video Ever*, Sony Wonder Video

Spot Goes to School, Where's Spot?, Spot Goes to a Party, etc.,
    Disney Video
The Very Hungry Caterpillar, Disney Video

OTHER FAVORITES

Barney Songs, Lyons (This longer-than-usual tape has 50 min-
    utes of sing-along songs and dances; there are many other
    good Barney selections including *Alphabet Zoo*, all from
    Lyons.)
Raffi in Concert, MCA
Sesame Street's Count It Higher, Sony Wonder Video (or many
    other *Sesame Street* choices, all Sony Wonder Video)
Wee Sing, MCA Video (Lots of parents recommend this series.)
Winnie the Pooh and the Blustery Day and many other Pooh
    titles, Disney Video

WHEN A NEW BABY IS ON THE WAY

Hey, What About Me, Kidvidz
A New Baby in My House, Sesame Street, Sony Wonder Video

Catalogs and References

Catalog shopping is a time-saver for busy grandparents, and also guarantees that gifts to distant grandchildren are returnable. You'll also find many ideas, and items that aren't readily available in stores.

ALL-PURPOSE CATALOGS

Request these two catalogs to get an idea of the wide range of children's products available. They include furniture, equipment, books, tapes and CDs, toys, safety items, and lots of things you probably never knew existed. It takes two to three weeks for most catalogs to arrive.

One Step Ahead
P.O. Box 517
Lake Bluff, IL 60044
(800) 274-8440

The Right Start
Right Start Plaza
5334 Sterling Center Drive
Westlake Village, CA 91361
(800) 548-8531
The Right Start also has stores in 16 states; check the catalog
for locations near you.

SAFETY

Perfectly Safe
7835 Freedom Avenue NW, Suite 3
North Canton, OH 44720
(800) 837-KIDS
Every kind of device to keep children safe from birth through
preschool years, with creative ideas like "tubbly-bubbly ele-
phant," a soft guard to prevent bumps from the bathtub faucet.
The catalog includes safe early toys.

CLOTHING

Children's catalogs include sizes from infant to teens; these
have many selections for babies and toddlers.

Biobottoms
617-C 2nd Street
Petaluma, CA 94952
(800) 766-1254

Natural fiber diaper covers and lots of adorable clothing for babies

Hanna Anderson
1010 NW Flanders
Portland, OR 97209
(800) 222-0544
High quality, Swedish-inspired designs in pure cotton

Lands' End Kids
1 Lands' End Lane
Dodgeville, WI 53595
(800) 356-4444
Clothes plus nap mats, sleeping bags, towels, and bedding

L. L. Bean Kids
Freeport, ME 04033
(800) 341-4341
Especially good for cold weather gear, including buntings

CHILDREN'S BOOKS

Chinaberry Book Service
2780 Via Orange Way, Suite B
Spring Valley, CA 91978
(800) 776-2242
Charming catalogs with quality selections for all ages and personal reviews of each book

TOYS (AND MORE)

Back to Basics Toys
31333 Agoura Road
Westlake Village, CA 91361
(800) 356-5360
Classics like blocks and construction toys, dollhouses, wooden
toy kitchens, puzzles, musical and crafts equipment

Birthday Express
11220 120th Avenue NE
Kirkland, WA 98033
(800) 424-7843
Pages of ideas for grandparents who want to lend a hand for
children's parties, plus gift toys to go with party themes. (Be
sure to check themes with parents before you proceed!) Some
of the favors make great small nonbirthday gifts for your own
grandchild.

Constructive Playthings
1227 119th Street
Grandview, MO 64030
(800) 832-0572
Toys for all ages plus tables and chairs, rocking horses, person-
alized shelves. Several pages are devoted to "first playthings."

Hand in Hand
891 Main Street
Oxford, ME 04270
(800) 872-9745
Everything for kids (including a mini-kitchen sink)—toys, books, puzzles, and some rather pricey but unique luggage and furniture

Learn and Play
45 Curiosity Lane, P.O. Box 1822
Peoria, IL 61656
(800) 247-6106
Mostly for older children, but several pages offer videos, alphabet and number games for preschoolers, and children's furniture, bedding, and storage items that make good gifts

Lilly's Kids
Lillian Vernon Corporation
Virginia Beach, VA 23479
(800) 285-5555
Great range of toys for all ages, plus accessories, bedding

Sensational Beginnings
P.O. Box 2009
987 Stewart Road
Monroe, MI 48162
(800) 444-2147
A section of toys for "The Wonder Years" has a wide selection

for preschoolers, including creative bath toys and a first indoor/outdoor playground.

This Country's Toys
P.O. Box 41479
Providence, RI 02940
(800) 359-1233
Sturdy toys made in America, with many offerings for infants and toddlers, and a wide selection of blocks and trains plus children's furniture

Toys to Grow On
P.O. Box 17
Long Beach, CA 90801
(800) 542-8338
A wide variety of toys from age three up, including a page of gift ideas under $10

MUSIC AND VIDEOS

Alcazar Music
P.O. Box 429, South Main Street
Waterbury, VT 05676
(800) 541-9904
Big catalog containing over 40 pages of children's Music and Storytelling tapes and CDs, another 25 pages of children's videos, with recommendations of their best-selling titles

CATALOGS AND REFERENCE BOOKS

These books are reliable sources for more detailed buying information:

Baby Stuff: A No-nonsense Shopping Guide for Every Parent's Lifestyle, Ari Lipper and Joanna Lipper, Dell Trade Paperback, Bantam Doubleday Dell Publishing Group, New York. Excellent guide to buying baby equipment.

Consumer Product Safety Division: A Grandparents Guide to Safety can be obtained by calling 1-888-8 PUEBLO.

Consumer Reports Guide to Baby Products, Consumer Reports Books, Yonkers, NY. Reports on quality and safety of baby equipment by this respected testing organization.

The Best Toys, Books & Videos for Kids, Joanne Oppenheim & Stephanie Oppenheim, published annually by Harper Perennial, Harper Collins, New York. A good guide to the basics as well as the newest options for various ages.

The Childwise Catalog, Jack Gillis and Mary Ellen R. Fise, Consumer Federation of America, Harper Perennial, New York. Comprehensive guide from equipment to toys, books and magazines for newborns to age five.

Picture Books for Children, Patricia J. Cianciolo, American Library Association, Chicago. This book of recommendations written by an educator is intended for librarians and costs $34, but may be of interest for grandparents who want to learn more about today's children's literature.

Information Sources

AARP Grandparent Information Center, 601 E Street, NW Washington, D.C. 20049, (202) 434-2296. A referral service for grandparents who find themselves raising grandchildren.

Club Med, (800) 258-2633. Offers family clubs with care facilities even for infants. A great bet for a two- or three-generation vacation.

The Foundation for Grandparenting, 5 Casa del Oro Lane, Santa Fe, NM 87505. An organization dedicated to grandparental concerns. It issues a quarterly newsletter and sponsors a summer grandparent-grandchild camp. Membership is $20 annually.

Grandtravel, (800) 247-7651. Trips for grandparents and grandchildren; file this one away until the kids are old enough to travel.

Internet Sites for Grandparents

The following parenting sites will be of interest to grandparents. Their exact offerings change frequently, and may differ slightly from this information. For more and newer Internet sources, use your browser to search for "grandparenting."

Parentsplace.com has numerous bulletin boards, including one devoted to grandparents, where both parents and grandparents can share problems and opinions.

Parentsoup.com has a weekly chat room for grandparents. Use their search space to find other areas of interest.

Uconnect.com/CGA/ offers articles and an on-line discussion on grandparenting topics.

OTHER BOOKS ON GRANDPARENTING

Becoming a Grandmother: A Life Transition, by Sheila Kitzinger, Scribner, 1996. A British writer looks at the transitions grandparenting brings.

Grandchildren Are So Much Fun, I Should Have Had Them First, Lois Wyse, Crown, 1992. Anecdotes from a veteran grandmother with a great sense of humor.

The Happy Helpful Grandma Guide, Leslie Lehr Spirson with Clair J. Lehr, Ph.D., Meadowbrook Press, 1995. A mother and grandmother share and compare their perceptions.

The Long Distance Grandmother, by Selma Wasserman, Hartley & Marks, 1996. A grandmother shares her firsthand experiences.

You Wouldn't Believe What My Grandchild Did . . . , Lois Wyse, Simon & Schuster, 1994. More of the same.

These books have helpful insights to share when your grandchild is older:

Contemporary Grandparenting, Arthur Kornhaber, M.D., Sage Publications, 1996

Grandparent Power, Arthur Kornhaber, M.D., with Sondra Forsyth, Crown, 1994

The Magic of Grandparenting, Charmaine L. Ciardi, Cathy Nikkel Orme, and Carolyn Quatrano, Henry Holt & Company, 1995

Other books that may be helpful with family relations:

Making Peace in Your Stepfamily, Dr. Harold H. Bloomfield, Hyperion, New York, 1994

—*Six in the Bed,* Nancy Cocola, Perigee Books, New York, 1997

Index